Weight Watchers®

Slim Ways™
Chicken

Macmillan • USA

SKU 3595400

MACMILLAN
A Prentice Hall Macmillan Company
15 Columbus Circle
New York, NY 10023

Library of Congress Cataloging-in-Publication Data
Weight Watchers slim ways chicken.
    p. cm.
    Includes index.
    ISBN 0–02–860364–8
    1. Reducing diets—Recipes. 2. Cookery (Chicken) I. Weight Watchers International.
RM222.2.W327   1995   94–24254
613.2'5—dc20   CIP

Manufactured in the United States of America

10 9 8 7 6 5 4 3 2 1

Contents

Weight Watchers

Since 1963, Weight Watchers has grown from a handful of people to millions of enrollments annually. Today, Weight Watchers is the recognized leading name in safe and sensible weight control. Weight Watchers members form a diverse group, from youths ten years old and older to senior citizens, attending meetings virtually around the globe.

Growing numbers of people purchase and enjoy our popular, expanding line of convenience foods, best-selling cookbooks, personal calendar planners and audio and video tapes. Weight-loss and weight-management results vary by the individual, but we recommend that you attend Weight Watchers meetings, follow the Weight Watchers food plan and participate in regular physical activity. For the Weight Watchers meeting nearest you, call 1-800-651-6000.

1

Chicken Chat

Chicken is truly a convenience food, available today in a wide variety of forms. Try boneless breasts, nuggets or cubes for shish kabob or strips for stir-frying, all of which have been trimmed to save you time. Here are some of the different types of chicken sold by butchers and grocers today:

Whole broiler-fryer: A thrifty way to buy chicken; usual weight is 3 to $4^1/_2$ pounds; packaged with or without neck and giblets.

Young roaster: A good choice for a crowd; large and meaty, usual weight is 5 to 8 pounds; a good source of cooked chicken for fast recipes; includes neck and giblets to save for making broth.

Capon: Surgically unsexed male broiler; usual weight is 8 to 10 pounds; suitable for roasting or poaching; very generous breast meat for recipes calling for cooked chicken, especially salads.

Rock Cornish game hen: Young chicken with the British breed Cornish in its blood line; usual weight is 1 to $1^1/_2$ pounds.

Hen: Adult female chicken; suitable for soup or stew.

Free-range chicken: Chicken that is raised on a farm and allowed unlimited access to area outside the coops. Usually comes from small flocks; eats only simple mixtures of grains found in the barnyard.

Cut-up chicken: Whole broiler cut into pieces; usual package contains 2 each of breast halves, thighs, drumsticks and wings; generally sold without giblets.

Halves or splits: Broiler cut into 2 equal pieces; good choice for grilling or broiling.

Quarters: Leg quarters consist of drumstick, thigh and back portion; all dark meat. Breast quarters include wing, breast and back portion; all white meat. Usually sold separately.

Leg: Whole leg with unseparated drumstick and thigh; all dark meat.

Thigh: Leg portion above the knee joint; available bone-in or skinless and boneless; all dark meat.

Drumstick: Lower portion of leg; all dark meat; ideal for finger food.

Breast halves or split breast: Usually the most expensive way to buy chicken but also the most meat for your money; available with or without bone and/or skin; all white meat.

Wings: Whole 3-section wing; frequently used for soup; all white meat.

Drummette: First section only of wing; good for hors d'oeuvres and finger food recipes; all white meat.

Ground chicken: Commercially ground chicken is usually dark meat; if the chicken is ground from the breast or wing only, the producer will usually label it "white meat." If the label says "chicken meat," it will be 100 percent chicken. If the label says "ground chicken," the product may contain ground skin in the same natural proportion as the chicken part from which it came.

How to cut up a whole chicken:

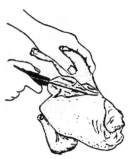

1. With breast side down, grasp chicken by legs. Using a sharp knife, remove wing by cutting close to body of chicken through joint attaching wing to breast. Reach around bird and remove second wing.

2. With legs toward you, place chicken on back on cutting board. Grasping one leg, cut skin between thigh and body to thigh joint.

3. Lifting chicken, bend leg back until thigh joint "pops." Cut around thigh joint to remove leg. Repeat on opposite side.

4. Separate thigh from drumstick by cutting through joint, removing the yellow line of fat.

5. To separate breast and back, set bird on neck end. Holding tail section, cut diagonally along rib cage to back bone.

6. Keeping knife very close to bone, cut along backbone through neck end. (Apply extra pressure as you cut through bones.) Repeat on opposite side to loosen back section completely.

7. Whole breast is ready to use as is or may be split. To split, place breast skin side down. Make a cut through V of wishbone. Bend breast back until keel bone "pops." Run thumb between meat and keel bone to loosen tissue. Pull bone from breast.

8. Split breast down the center. Halves may be boned if desired.

Here is a simple technique for boning chicken thighs in three easy steps.

1. Cut along thin side, joint to joint.

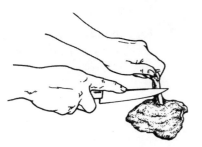

2. Cut meat from one joint. Then pull or scrape meat from bone.

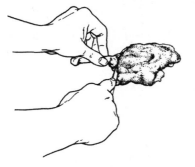

3. Cut meat from other joint.

Boning half a chicken breast

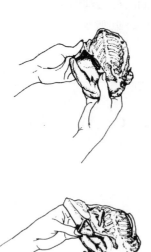

1. Holding breast half in both hands, bend and break keel bone.

2. Run thumb between meat and keel bone, removing the bone and strip of cartilage.

3. Using both thumbs, loosen meat from rib cage.

4. Pull or scrape breast meat away from bones. (If small pieces of wishbone remain, pull them out or cut away with knife.)

HOW TO BUY AND STORE CHICKEN

Buying Tips

Check the "sell by" date on the package labels. This date indicates the last day the product should be offered for sale, but the chicken will maintain its high quality if properly refrigerated and cooked within a few days.

How Much to Buy

Before deciding how much chicken to buy, you need to determine how many ounces of cooked chicken you want to end up with. For whole or cut-up chicken, multiply the desired cooked amount by 3. For example, if you want to end up with 12 ounces cooked chicken (edible portion), you should buy 2¼ pounds whole or cut-up chicken.

For parts with skin and bone, such as breasts, whole legs, drumsticks and thighs, multiply edible cooked weight by 2. For example, if you want to end up with 12 ounces cooked chicken, buy 1½ pounds chicken parts. For skinless, boneless chicken, such as breasts or thighs, allow 1 ounce shrinkage per 4 ounces; for example, 4 ounces of raw skinless boneless chicken will yield about 3 ounces cooked.

Storage Tips

All poultry is perishable. Care should be taken in the handling, preparation, cooking and serving of poultry products. Place the package on a plate in the refrigerator to prevent juices from dripping onto other foods. Refrigerate fresh poultry promptly in the coldest area of your refrigerator if you are planning to use it within a day or two. Never leave poultry unrefrigerated for more than 2 hours.

For longer storage, freeze poultry in moisture-vapor-proof materials such as aluminum foil, freezer wrap or freezer bags. Press all air out of the package before sealing. Be careful not to puncture the wrap with bones or sharp wing tips. Seal and label packages with contents, weight and date. Rotate your inventory, always using the oldest packages first. It is not recommended that either cooked or uncooked chicken be refrozen once it has thawed.

	Refrigerator (40° F)	Freezer (0° F)
Fresh raw chicken		
Whole chicken	1–2 days	1 year
Chicken parts	1–2 days	9 months
Giblets	1–2 days	3–4 months
Ground chicken	1–2 days	3–4 months
Cooked chicken, leftovers		
Whole roasted chicken	3–4 days	4 months
Cooked chicken dishes	3–4 days	4–6 months
Chicken parts (plain)	3–4 days	4 months
Parts with gravy, broth	1–2 days	6 months
Chicken nuggets, cubes, patties	1–2 days	1–3 months

Thaw frozen items in the refrigerator (a 4-pound whole chicken will take approximately 24 hours; cut-up parts, 4 to 9 hours) or follow package directions for defrosting in the microwave. To thaw poultry quickly, fill a bowl with cold water. Add still-wrapped chicken and change water frequently. A whole 4-pound chicken will take about 4 hours to thaw. Use promptly when defrosted.

HOW TO HANDLE CHICKEN SAFELY

Always wash your hands, countertops and utensils in hot, soapy water before and after each step of chicken preparation. Do not use the knife or cutting board for other foods until you have washed them thoroughly. Always use a clean platter for serving cooked chicken, never the same one that has held the raw poultry.

Cooking Tips

The USDA recommends cooking boneless chicken to an internal temperature of 160° F, and whole chicken or bone-in cut-up parts to 180° F. If you are not using a thermometer, cook poultry until juices are clear, not pink.

Healthful Tips

Chicken is naturally nutritious, but your cooking methods can make it even healthier for you:

- Almost half the fat in chicken is found in the skin. Remove it before or after cooking.
- Trim all visible fat before preparation.
- Season with calorie-free herbs and spices, flavored vinegars or citrus juices instead of sauces.
- Choose low-sodium ingredients to prepare your recipes.
- Broil, roast, bake, grill or poach chicken. Sauté in a small amount of chicken broth or use nonstick cooking spray.
- Keep your side dishes healthy too! Serve natural grains and fresh steamed vegetables with chicken, and have fresh fruit for dessert.

Chicken Nutrition Chart

	Cal (kcal)	Pro (g)	Total Fat (g)	Sat Fat (g)	Chol (mg)	Sod (mg)
Breast	116	24	2	0	72	63
Drumstick	131	23	4	1	79	81
Thigh	152	21	7	2	81	75
Whole	134	23	4	1	76	73
Wing	147	23	6	2	72	78

Serving size: 3 ounces cooked skinless edible portion; roasted, broiled, grilled, microwaved, stir-fried, poached, simmered; without additional fat, salt or sauces.

2

Fun Finger Foods

Buffalo Chicken Wings
Curried Chicken Wings
Chicken Wings Cacciatore
Sweet and Spicy Wings
Chicken Wings in Black Bean Sauce
Tailgate Chicken
Picnic Drumsticks
Honey-Mustard Drumsticks
Crunchy Chicken Nuggets
Deviled Chicken
Western ChickChunks
Jerk Chicken
Chicken-Cheese Rolls
Apricot-Chicken Roll-Ups
Blue Cheese–Chicken Burgers
Chicken Burgers on Toasted Sourdough Bread
Chicken Croquettes
Chicken Sloppy Joes
Chicken Club Sandwiches
Chicken Tabbouleh Pockets
Homemade Pizza
Special Pizza Additions
Chicken Reuben
Chicken-Pineapple Kabobs

BUFFALO CHICKEN WINGS

Make these wings just as hot as you like by adjusting the amount of hot pepper sauce. Hot fruit sauce, such as PickaPeppa® sauce, is available in many supermarkets and gourmet stores; if you can't find it, substitute aromatic bitters.

Makes 4 servings

- 2 tablespoons hot fruit sauce
- 1 tablespoon hot pepper sauce, or to taste
- 1 tablespoon + 1 teaspoon corn oil
- 2 pounds 4 ounces roaster chicken-wing drumsticks, skinned*

- ½ cup skim buttermilk
- 1½ ounces blue cheese, crumbled
- ¼ teaspoon black pepper
- 8 medium celery stalks, cut into sticks

1. Preheat oven to 450° F. Line large baking sheet with foil; spray with non-stick cooking spray.
2. In medium bowl, combine hot fruit sauce, hot pepper sauce and oil; add chicken, tossing to coat thoroughly. Place chicken in a single layer on prepared baking sheet, reserving any remaining hot pepper sauce mixture. Bake 15–20 minutes, turning once, until chicken is cooked through and lightly browned, basting occasionally with reserved hot pepper sauce mixture.
3. While chicken is baking, in small bowl, combine buttermilk, blue cheese and black pepper. Serve hot chicken wings and celery sticks with buttermilk mixture as a dip.

Each serving provides: 1 Fat; 1 Vegetable; 3½ Proteins; 20 Optional Calories

Per serving: 284 Calories; 30 g Protein; 15 g Fat; 6 g Carbohydrate; 130 mg Calcium; 457 mg Sodium; 81 mg Cholesterol; 1 g Dietary Fiber

*Roaster chicken wings, with the drumstick portion already separated from the lower part of the wing, are available in the meat section of the supermarket. Freeze the lower part to have on hand when making chicken broth.

CURRIED CHICKEN WINGS

Delicious and messy to eat, these mildly spiced meaty wing portions are great served with chutney and rice pilaf.

Makes 4 servings

1 tablespoon + 1 teaspoon peanut oil

2 tablespoons mild or hot curry powder

2 teaspoons ground cumin

2 teaspoons dried oregano leaves

1 teaspoon ground coriander seed

1 teaspoon ground cardamom

1 teaspoon ground ginger

1 teaspoon salt

½ teaspoon black pepper

¼ teaspoon ground red pepper

¾ cup plain nonfat yogurt

1 tablespoon + 1 teaspoon honey

2 pounds 4 ounces roaster chicken-wing drumsticks, skinned*

1. In small skillet, heat oil; add curry powder, cumin, oregano, coriander, cardamom, ginger, salt, black pepper and ground red pepper. Cook over low heat, stirring constantly, 15 minutes. Transfer seasoning mixture to small bowl; with wire whisk, stir in yogurt and honey.
2. Spoon yogurt mixture into gallon-size sealable plastic bag; add chicken. Seal bag, squeezing out air; turn to coat chicken. Refrigerate at least 6 hours or overnight, turning bag occasionally.
3. Preheat oven to 450° F. Line large baking sheet with foil; spray with nonstick cooking spray.
4. With tongs, arrange chicken in a single layer on prepared baking sheet. Spoon any remaining sauce evenly over chicken. Bake 15–20 minutes, until chicken is cooked through and golden brown.

Each serving provides: ¼ Milk; 1 Fat; 3 Proteins; 20 Optional Calories

Per serving: 280 Calories; 29 g Protein; 12 g Fat; 13 g Carbohydrate; 143 mg Calcium; 665 mg Sodium; 73 mg Cholesterol; 1 g Dietary Fiber

*Roaster chicken wings, with the drumstick portion already separated from the lower part of the wing, are available in the meat section of the supermarket. Freeze the lower part to have on hand when making chicken broth.

CHICKEN WINGS CACCIATORE

Makes 4 servings

1 tablespoon + 1 teaspoon olive oil

2 pounds 4 ounces roaster chicken-wing drumsticks, skinned*

3 cups thickly sliced mushrooms

1 cup diced onions

1 tablespoon minced fresh garlic

1½ cups chopped canned Italian tomatoes (reserve juice)

½ cup (4 fluid ounces) dry red wine

2 teaspoons red wine vinegar

1 teaspoon dried oregano leaves

½ teaspoon dried rosemary leaves

½ teaspoon coarsely ground black pepper

½ teaspoon salt

½ teaspoon crushed red pepper flakes (optional)

1. In large skillet, heat 2 teaspoons of the oil; add chicken. Cook over medium-high heat 2 minutes on each side, until golden brown. Remove chicken from skillet; set aside.

2. In same skillet, heat remaining 2 teaspoons oil; add mushrooms and onions. Cook, stirring frequently, until liquid has evaporated and vegetables are golden brown. Add garlic; cook, stirring constantly, 1 minute longer.

3. Add tomatoes with juice, wine, vinegar, oregano, rosemary, black pepper, salt and crushed red pepper, if using; bring to a boil. Return chicken to skillet; stir to coat. Reduce heat to low; simmer, covered, 20 minutes, stirring occasionally. Remove cover; simmer 15–20 minutes longer, until liquid is reduced slightly.

Each serving provides: 1 Fat; 2¾ Vegetables; 3 Proteins; 25 Optional Calories

Per serving: 286 Calories; 29 g Protein; 12 g Fat; 12 g Carbohydrate; 65 mg Calcium; 504 mg Sodium; 72 mg Cholesterol; 2 g Dietary Fiber

Roaster chicken wings, with the drumstick portion already separated from the lower part of the wing, are available in the meat section of the supermarket. Freeze the lower part to have on hand when making chicken broth.

SWEET AND SPICY WINGS

Makes 4 servings

1 tablespoon + 1 teaspoon stick margarine

½ cup minced onion

1 tablespoon minced fresh garlic

2 teaspoons ground ginger

1 teaspoon salt

1 teaspoon paprika

¾ teaspoon dried sage leaves

½ teaspoon ground cumin

¼ teaspoon ground red pepper, or to taste

¼ cup (2 fluid ounces) dry sherry

3 tablespoons honey

2 pounds 4 ounces roaster chicken-wing drumsticks, skinned*

1. Preheat oven to 300° F. Spray a 13 × 9" baking pan with nonstick cooking spray.
2. In small skillet, heat margarine; add onion and garlic. Cook over low heat, stirring constantly, 5 minutes, until soft. Add ginger, salt, paprika, sage, cumin and ground red pepper; cook, stirring constantly, 1 minute. Add sherry and honey; mix well.
3. Place chicken in prepared baking pan; coat thoroughly with sherry mixture. Bake 1 hour, basting often, until chicken is cooked through and begins to brown.
4. To serve, transfer chicken to serving platter; top with pan juices.

Each serving provides: 1 Fat; ¼ Vegetable; 3 Proteins; 60 Optional Calories

Per serving: 297 Calories; 27 g Protein; 11 g Fat; 19 g Carbohydrate; 36 mg Calcium; 677 mg Sodium; 73 mg Cholesterol; 0 g Dietary Fiber

*Roaster chicken wings, with the drumstick portion already separated from the lower part of the wing, are available in the meat section of the supermarket. Freeze the lower part to have on hand when making chicken broth.

CHICKEN WINGS IN BLACK BEAN SAUCE

Makes 4 servings

1 medium scallion, minced and crushed

1 tablespoon soaked, rinsed, drained and crushed fermented black beans*

1 tablespoon minced pared fresh ginger root

3 garlic cloves, crushed

1 pound 8 ounces roaster chicken-wing drumsticks, skinned†

1 cup low-sodium chicken broth

⅓ cup dry sherry

¼ cup oyster sauce†

2 tablespoons granulated sugar

1 medium green bell pepper, seeded and cubed

2 teaspoons cornstarch, dissolved in 1 tablespoon cold water

1. In medium bowl, combine scallion, black beans, ginger and garlic; add chicken, tossing well to coat thoroughly. Refrigerate, covered, at least 2 hours or overnight.

2. In medium saucepan, combine broth, sherry, oyster sauce and sugar; bring to a boil. Add chicken mixture; reduce heat to low. Cook, covered, 15 minutes. Stir in green pepper; cook, covered, 10 minutes longer, until chicken is cooked through. Stir in dissolved cornstarch; cook, stirring constantly, 1 minute, until slightly thickened.

Each serving provides: ½ Vegetable; 2 Proteins; 85 Optional Calories

Per serving: 173 Calories; 16 g Protein; 3 g Fat; 16 g Carbohydrate; 25 mg Calcium; 878 mg Sodium; 32 mg Cholesterol; 0 g Dietary Fiber

*Fermented black beans can be purchased in jars or bags in Asian food stores or the Asian food section of some supermarkets. Don't confuse them with dried black (turtle) beans. Fermented black beans need to be soaked briefly before using. They lend a distinctive salty flavor to dishes.

†Roaster chicken wings, with the drumstick portion already separated from the lower part of the wing, are available in the meat section of the supermarket. Freeze the lower part to have on hand when making chicken broth.

‡Oyster sauce, a thick, dark sauce made of oyster extract and salt, imparts a rich flavor to dishes. It can be purchased in Asian food stores or the Asian food section of some supermarkets.

TAILGATE CHICKEN

Serve these spicy drumsticks with baked beans or macaroni salad.

Makes 4 servings

2 tablespoons smooth peanut butter

1 tablespoon + 1 teaspoon honey

1 tablespoon hot pepper sauce

1 tablespoon low-sodium chicken broth

2 garlic cloves, mashed into a purée

1 teaspoon low-sodium soy sauce

Four 6-ounce chicken drumsticks, skinned

½ cup + 1 tablespoon plain dried bread crumbs

1 teaspoon paprika

⅛ teaspoon ground red pepper (optional)

1. Preheat oven to 400° F. Line large baking sheet with foil; spray with non-stick cooking spray.
2. In large bowl, combine peanut butter, honey, hot pepper sauce, broth, garlic and soy sauce. Add chicken, tossing well to coat thoroughly.
3. In gallon-size sealable plastic bag, combine bread crumbs, paprika and ground red pepper, if using; seal bag and shake to blend. Add 1 chicken drumstick; seal bag and shake to coat. Place coated chicken drumstick on prepared baking sheet; repeat, using remaining chicken drumsticks.
4. Bake chicken 20 minutes; turn carefully. Bake 15 minutes longer, until cooked through and juices run clear when pierced with a fork.

Each serving provides: ½ Fat; 3½ Proteins; ¾ Bread; 40 Optional Calories

Per serving: 283 Calories; 29 g Protein; 10 g Fat; 19 g Carbohydrate; 52 mg Calcium; 399 mg Sodium; 79 mg Cholesterol; 1 g Dietary Fiber

PICNIC DRUMSTICKS

Makes 4 servings

Four 6-ounce chicken drumsticks, skinned

¼ cup fat-free Catalina-style dressing

⅓ cup + 2 teaspoons plain dried bread crumbs

1 teaspoon paprika

½ teaspoon dried oregano leaves

⅛ teaspoon ground red pepper

1. Preheat oven to 400° F. Line large baking sheet with foil; spray with non-stick cooking spray.
2. In large bowl, combine chicken and dressing, tossing to coat thoroughly.
3. In gallon-size sealable plastic bag, combine bread crumbs, paprika, oregano and ground red pepper; seal bag and shake to blend. Add 1 drumstick; seal bag and shake to coat. Place drumstick on prepared baking sheet. Repeat, using remaining drumsticks. Bake 25–35 minutes, until chicken is cooked through and juices run clear when pierced with a fork.

Each serving provides: 3 Proteins; ½ Bread; 20 Optional Calories

Per serving: 206 Calories; 25 g Protein; 6 g Fat; 11 g Carbohydrate; 37 mg Calcium; 288 mg Sodium; 79 mg Cholesterol; 0 g Dietary Fiber

HONEY–MUSTARD DRUMSTICKS

Makes 4 servings

¼ cup Dijon-style mustard

2 tablespoons + 2 teaspoons honey

2 tablespoons apple cider

Four 6-ounce chicken drum-sticks, skinned

⅓ cup + 2 teaspoons plain dried bread crumbs

1 teaspoon dry mustard

½ teaspoon salt

¼ teaspoon ground ginger

1. Preheat oven to 375° F. Line large baking sheet with foil; spray with non-stick cooking spray.

2. In large bowl, combine Dijon mustard, honey and cider; remove and set aside ¼ cup of mixture. To remaining mixture, add chicken, tossing well to coat thoroughly.

3. In gallon-size sealable plastic bag, combine bread crumbs, dry mustard, salt and ginger; seal bag and shake to blend. Add 1 drumstick; seal bag and shake to coat. Place drumstick on prepared baking sheet. Repeat, using remaining drumsticks.

4. Bake chicken 20 minutes; turn carefully. Bake 10–15 minutes longer, until cooked through and juices run clear when pierced with a fork. Serve with reserved mustard mixture as a dip.

Each serving provides: 3 Proteins; ½ Bread; 45 Optional Calories

Per serving: 256 Calories; 25 g Protein; 7 g Fat; 22 g Carbohydrate; 38 mg Calcium; 893 mg Sodium; 79 mg Cholesterol; 0 g Dietary Fiber

CRUNCHY CHICKEN NUGGETS

These tasty tidbits cook up in minutes and appeal to people of all ages!

Makes 4 servings

⅓ cup + 2 teaspoons unsweetened wheat germ

1 teaspoon paprika

½ teaspoon coarsely ground black pepper

¼ teaspoon salt

15 ounces skinless boneless chicken breasts, cut into bite-size pieces

2 teaspoons vegetable oil

1. In gallon-size sealable plastic bag, combine wheat germ, paprika, pepper and salt; seal bag and shake to blend. Add 3–4 chicken pieces; do not crowd bag. Seal bag and shake to coat. Place coated chicken pieces on large plate; repeat, using remaining chicken pieces.

2. In large nonstick skillet, heat oil; add coated chicken pieces. Cook, turning as needed, 10–12 minutes, until golden brown on all sides and cooked through.

Each serving provides: ½ Fat; 3 Proteins; ½ Bread

Per serving: 180 Calories; 28 g Protein; 5 g Fat; 6 g Carbohydrate; 20 mg Calcium; 205 mg Sodium; 62 mg Cholesterol; 1 g Dietary Fiber

DEVILED CHICKEN

This oven-fried chicken is crunchy and as spicy as you want it to be. Enjoy it hot or cold.

Makes 8 servings

2 teaspoons dry mustard (optional)

¼ cup Dijon-style mustard

2 garlic cloves, mashed into a purée

One 3-pound chicken, skinned and cut into 8 pieces

½ cup + 1 tablespoon plain dried bread crumbs

½ teaspoon dried thyme leaves

½ teaspoon black pepper

¼ teaspoon salt

⅛ teaspoon ground red pepper (optional)

1. In large bowl, combine dry mustard, if using, and 1 teaspoon cold water; stir well until mustard is dissolved. Let stand 30 minutes.
2. Preheat oven to 400° F. Line large baking sheet with foil; spray with non-stick cooking spray.
3. Add Dijon mustard and garlic to dissolved dry mustard; stir to combine. Add chicken, tossing well to coat thoroughly.
4. In gallon-size sealable plastic bag, combine bread crumbs, thyme, black pepper, salt and ground red pepper, if using; seal bag and shake to blend. Add 1 chicken piece; seal bag and shake to coat. Place coated chicken piece on prepared baking sheet; repeat, using remaining chicken pieces.
5. Bake 15 minutes; turn chicken over. Bake 10–15 minutes longer, until chicken is golden brown and cooked through and juices run clear when pierced with a fork.

Each serving provides: 2 Proteins; ¼ Bread; 10 Optional Calories

Per serving: 148 Calories; 17 g Protein; 5 g Fat; 7 g Carbohydrate; 30 mg Calcium; 407 mg Sodium; 50 mg Cholesterol; 0 g Dietary Fiber

WESTERN CHICKCHUNKS

Kids will just love to help prepare this dish. Serve with coleslaw or a salad, and a frosty frozen yogurt shake.

Makes 4 servings

10 ounces skinless boneless chicken breasts, cut into 12 equal pieces

¼ cup fat-free ranch dressing

¼ cup + 1 tablespoon cornflake crumbs

¼ teaspoon salt

¼ teaspoon black pepper

1. Preheat oven to 450° F. Line large baking sheet with foil; spray with nonstick cooking spray.
2. In small bowl, combine chicken and ranch dressing, tossing well to coat thoroughly. On shallow plate or in gallon-size sealable plastic bag, combine cornflake crumbs, salt and pepper. One at a time, add chicken pieces to crumb mixture, turning chicken or sealing bag and shaking to coat evenly.
3. Arrange chicken pieces on the prepared baking sheet; bake 15–20 minutes, until cooked through and juices run clear when pierced with a fork.

Each serving provides: 2 Proteins; ¼ Bread; 20 Optional Calories

Per serving: 117 Calories; 17 g Protein; 1 g Fat; 8 g Carbohydrate; 9 mg Calcium; 397 mg Sodium; 41 mg Cholesterol; 0 g Dietary Fiber

JERK CHICKEN

"Jerk" is a technique that was devised in Jamaica to preserve meat. The unique combination of spices has made it an international favorite.

Makes 4 servings

¼ cup (2 fluid ounces) dry red wine

½ medium jalapeño pepper, seeded and minced

2 tablespoons minced scallions

1 tablespoon + 1 teaspoon vegetable oil

1 tablespoon ground allspice

1 garlic clove, minced

1½ teaspoons ground coriander

½ teaspoon cinnamon

½ teaspoon low-sodium soy sauce

¼ teaspoon nutmeg

Four 4-ounce skinless boneless chicken breasts

1. In small bowl, combine wine, jalapeño pepper, scallions, oil, allspice, garlic, coriander, cinnamon, soy sauce and nutmeg, mixing to form a paste. Rub chicken evenly with seasoning paste; refrigerate, covered, at least 8 hours or overnight.
2. Preheat broiler. Broil chicken 6" from heat, 3½ minutes on each side, until cooked through.

Each serving provides: 1 Fat; 3 Proteins; 15 Optional Calories

Per serving: 184 Calories; 26 g Protein; 6 g Fat; 2 g Carbohydrate; 33 mg Calcium; 102 mg Sodium; 66 mg Cholesterol; 0 g Dietary Fiber

Chicken-Cheese Rolls

Makes 4 servings

Four 3-ounce skinless boneless
    chicken breasts

1 teaspoon olive oil

2 tablespoons minced onion

4 sun-dried tomato halves (not
    packed in oil), minced, soaked
    in hot water and drained

⅓ cup nonfat ricotta cheese

1½ ounces finely diced fontina
    cheese

2 tablespoons minced fresh
    flat-leaf parsley

¼ teaspoon dried oregano leaves

¼ teaspoon salt

⅛ teaspoon black pepper

2 tablespoons reduced-calorie
    tub margarine, melted

1 tablespoon skim milk

4 sheets frozen phyllo dough,
    thawed

1. Adjust oven racks to divide oven into thirds; preheat oven to 375° F. Line large baking sheet with foil; spray with nonstick cooking spray.
2. Place each chicken breast between 2 sheets of plastic wrap; with meat mallet, pound lightly to make thin, even ovals. Set chicken aside.
3. In small skillet, heat oil; add onion. Cook over medium heat, stirring frequently, 2–3 minutes, until soft. Transfer onion to small bowl; stir in tomatoes, ricotta and fontina cheeses, parsley, oregano, salt and pepper.
4. Spoon ¼ of the ricotta cheese mixture onto each chicken oval; fold sides of chicken over mixture, then roll up to enclose.
5. In a small bowl, combine margarine and milk. Brush 1 phyllo sheet with ⅛ of the margarine mixture, then fold sheet in half. Place 1 chicken roll at one end of sheet; fold sides of sheet over chicken, then roll up to enclose. Repeat, making 3 more rolls.
6. Place rolls on prepared baking sheet; brush with remaining margarine mixture. Bake in upper third of oven 25–30 minutes, until chicken is cooked through and crust is golden brown.

Each serving provides: 1 Fat; ½ Vegetable; 2¾ Proteins; ½ Bread;
    15 Optional Calories

Per serving: 258 Calories; 27 g Protein; 10 g Fat; 14 g Carbohydrate;
    184 mg Calcium; 452 mg Sodium; 62 mg Cholesterol; 1 g Dietary
    Fiber

APRICOT-CHICKEN ROLL-UPS

This dish is pretty enough for a party and couldn't be easier! Try it with orange spreadable fruit for a change of pace.

Makes 4 servings

3 tablespoons seasoned dried bread crumbs

Four 3-ounce skinless boneless chicken breasts, pounded thin

2 teaspoons canola oil

¼ cup apricot spreadable fruit, melted

1. Preheat broiler. Spray broiler pan with nonstick cooking spray.
2. Place bread crumbs on large sheet of wax paper. Brush 1 side of each chicken breast with ½ teaspoon of the oil; place oiled-side down on bread crumbs, pressing firmly to coat.
3. Brush uncoated side of each chicken breast with one-fourth of the spreadable fruit. Roll breasts to enclose fruit; secure with wooden toothpicks. Place chicken rolls in prepared broiler pan; broil 4" from heat 6–8 minutes, until cooked through.

Each serving provides: ½ Fat; 1 Fruit; 2 Proteins; ¼ Bread

Per serving: 178 Calories; 20 g Protein; 4 g Fat; 14 g Carbohydrate; 15 mg Calcium; 204 mg Sodium; 49 mg Cholesterol; 0 g Dietary Fiber

BLUE CHEESE-CHICKEN BURGERS

Makes 4 servings

10 ounces ground chicken

1 cup chopped scallions

1½ ounces blue cheese, crumbled

3 tablespoons plain dried bread crumbs

2 teaspoons Dijon-style mustard

⅛ teaspoon freshly ground black pepper

4 lettuce leaves

Four 1-ounce pitas, split and toasted

1. Preheat broiler. Spray rack in broiler pan with nonstick cooking spray.

2. In medium bowl, combine chicken, scallions, blue cheese, bread crumbs, Dijon mustard and pepper; shape evenly into 4 patties. Place patties on prepared rack; broil 4" from heat 5 minutes on each side, until cooked through.
3. To serve, layer 1 lettuce leaf and 1 patty on 1 pita half; top with another pita half. Repeat, making 3 more burgers.

Each serving provides: ¾ Vegetable; 2½ Proteins; 1¼ Breads

Per serving: 259 Calories; 18 g Protein; 10 g Fat; 22 g Carbohydrate; 134 mg Calcium; 481 mg Sodium; 67 mg Cholesterol; 1 g Dietary Fiber

CHICKEN BURGERS ON TOASTED SOURDOUGH BREAD

Makes 4 servings

14 ounces ground chicken
½ cup + 1 tablespoon seasoned dried bread crumbs
1 egg, lightly beaten
2 teaspoons Worcestershire sauce
3 drops hot pepper sauce, or to taste

Four 1-ounce diagonal slices sourdough bread, toasted
4 lettuce leaves
2 tablespoons + 2 teaspoons sweet pickle relish

1. In medium bowl, combine chicken, bread crumbs, egg, and Worcestershire and hot pepper sauces lightly but thoroughly; shape mixture into 4 equal patties.
2. Spray large nonstick skillet with nonstick cooking spray; place over medium heat. Add chicken patties; cook, turning once, 10–12 minutes, until golden brown and cooked through.
3. To serve, top each slice of bread with 1 lettuce leaf; place 1 cooked chicken patty and 2 teaspoons of the pickle relish onto each leaf.

Each serving provides: ¼ Vegetable; 3 Proteins; 1¾ Breads; 10 Optional Calories

Per serving: 331 Calories; 24 g Protein; 12 g Fat; 31 g Carbohydrate; 78 mg Calcium; 819 mg Sodium; 135 mg Cholesterol; 1 g Dietary Fiber

CHICKEN CROQUETTES

Makes 8 servings

Croquettes:

1 tablespoon vegetable oil

2 tablespoons minced onion

1 tablespoon minced celery

¾ cup low-sodium chicken broth

¾ cup evaporated skimmed milk

2 tablespoons all-purpose flour

½ teaspoon salt

½ teaspoon black pepper

Pinch ground red pepper

Pinch nutmeg

12 ounces skinless cooked chicken breast, minced

⅓ cup + 2 teaspoons plain dried bread crumbs

2 teaspoons unsalted butter*

Mushroom Sauce:

1 teaspoon vegetable oil

1 cup sliced mushrooms

2 tablespoons low-sodium chicken broth

1 teaspoon Dijon-style mustard

1. To prepare croquettes, in medium saucepan, heat 1 teaspoon of the oil; add onion and celery. Cook over medium heat, stirring frequently, until soft. In small bowl, with wire whisk, combine broth, milk and flour, blending until flour is dissolved. Strain and add to onion mixture; cook, stirring constantly, until mixture comes just to a boil. Reduce heat to low; stir in salt, black pepper, ground red pepper and nutmeg. Simmer 10 minutes, stirring frequently.

2. Transfer ¾ cup milk mixture to medium bowl; set remaining milk mixture aside. Stir chicken into milk mixture in bowl. With moistened fingers, form mixture into sixteen 2" patties (about 2 level tablespoons each). Place bread crumbs on shallow plate; add patties gently, turning to coat.

3. In large nonstick skillet, heat the remaining 2 teaspoons oil and butter; when foam subsides, add coated chicken patties. Cook patties until golden brown on both sides. Transfer croquettes to serving platter; keep warm.

4. To prepare mushroom sauce, in medium saucepan, heat oil; add mushrooms. Cook over medium heat, stirring frequently, 5 minutes, until mushrooms release their juices; stir in reserved milk mixture, broth and Dijon mustard. Bring mixture just to a boil; reduce heat to low. Cook, stirring frequently, 5 minutes. Serve with croquettes.

Each serving provides: ¼ Milk; ½ Fat; ¼ Vegetable; 1½ Proteins; ¼ Bread; 20 Optional Calories

Per serving: 152 Calories; 16 g Protein; 5 g Fat; 9 g Carbohydrate; 91 mg Calcium; 265 mg Sodium; 40 mg Cholesterol; 0 g Dietary Fiber

*Stick margarine may be substituted for the butter; increase Fat Selection to ¾ and reduce Optional Calories to 10.

Per serving with stick margarine: 152 Calories; 16 g Protein; 5 g Fat; 9 g Carbohydrate; 91 mg Calcium; 276 mg Sodium; 37 mg Cholesterol; 0 g Dietary Fiber

CHICKEN SLOPPY JOES

Makes 4 servings

1 tablespoon + 1 teaspoon margarine	¼ cup low-sodium chicken broth
½ cup chopped celery	3 tablespoons chili sauce
½ cup chopped onion	¼ teaspoon mild or hot chili powder
½ cup diced green bell pepper	Four 2-ounce hamburger rolls, split and lightly toasted
½ cup diced red bell pepper	
10 ounces skinless cooked chicken, shredded	

1. In large nonstick skillet, melt margarine; add celery, onion and green and red peppers. Cook, stirring frequently, 4–5 minutes, until vegetables are tender.
2. Add chicken, broth, chili sauce and chili powder to vegetable mixture; bring liquid to a boil. Reduce heat to low; simmer 2 minutes, until heated through. Spoon evenly over hamburger rolls.

Each serving provides: 1 Fat; 1 Vegetable; 2½ Proteins; 2 Breads; 15 Optional Calories

Per serving: 363 Calories; 26 g Protein; 12 g Fat; 36 g Carbohydrate; 106 mg Calcium; 613 mg Sodium; 63 mg Cholesterol; 2 g Dietary Fiber

Chicken Club Sandwiches

These hearty, mile-high sandwiches go nicely with crunchy pickles, carrots and your favorite olives.

Makes 4 servings

2 tablespoons + 2 teaspoons reduced-calorie mayonnaise

1 tablespoon pickle relish

1 tablespoon fresh lemon juice

⅛ teaspoon freshly ground black pepper

Four 3-ounce skinless boneless chicken breasts, pounded thin

12 slices reduced-calorie white bread, toasted

8 lettuce leaves

2 medium tomatoes, cut into 8 slices

4 slices crisp-cooked turkey bacon (30 calories per slice)

1. Preheat broiler. Spray rack in broiler pan with nonstick cooking spray.
2. In small bowl, combine mayonnaise, relish, lemon juice and pepper; set aside.
3. Place chicken on prepared rack; broil 6" from heat 3½ minutes on each side, until cooked through. Let chicken cool slightly.
4. Spread mayonnaise mixture evenly on each slice of toast. Layer 1 slice of toast, mayonnaise-side up, with 1 lettuce leaf, 2 tomato slices, 1 bacon slice, another slice of toast, another lettuce leaf, 1 chicken breast and a third slice of toast, mayonnaise-side down; repeat, making 3 more sandwiches. Serve sandwiches cut in half diagonally.

Each serving provides: 1 Fat; 1½ Vegetables; 2 Proteins; 1½ Breads; 35 Optional Calories

Per serving: 323 Calories; 29 g Protein; 8 g Fat; 37 g Carbohydrate; 90 mg Calcium; 643 mg Sodium; 62 mg Cholesterol; 8 g Dietary Fiber

CHICKEN TABBOULEH POCKETS

Here's a fresh taste from the Middle East—and a great way to use up leftover cooked chicken.

Makes 4 servings

4 ounces uncooked bulgur (cracked wheat)

3 tablespoons fresh lemon juice

1 tablespoon + 1 teaspoon olive oil

½ teaspoon dried oregano leaves

¼ teaspoon salt

¼ teaspoon freshly ground black pepper

8 ounces skinless cooked chicken, cubed

½ cup chopped tomato

¼ cup golden raisins

2 tablespoons chopped fresh cilantro

Two 2-ounce pitas, halved crosswise to form 4 pockets

4 romaine lettuce leaves

1. In medium bowl, combine bulgur and 1 cup boiling water; let stand 30 minutes. Drain thoroughly any excess water; return bulgur to bowl.
2. In small bowl, with wire whisk, combine lemon juice, oil, oregano, salt and pepper. Pour over bulgur; toss well to coat thoroughly. Add chicken, tomato, raisins and cilantro; toss to combine.
3. To serve, line each pita pocket with 1 lettuce leaf; spoon one-fourth of the chicken mixture into each pocket.

Each serving provides: 1 Fat; ½ Fruit; ½ Vegetable; 2 Proteins; 2 Breads

Per serving: 359 Calories; 23 g Protein; 10 g Fat; 47 g Carbohydrate; 57 mg Calcium; 345 mg Sodium; 50 mg Cholesterol; 7 g Dietary Fiber

Homemade Pizza

This pizza is limited only by your imagination. Top it with one or more varieties of cheese, such as mozzarella, feta, cheddar or Parmesan, and then crown it with a Special Pizza Addition from the selection that follows. Once you've made your own pizza, you'll never call for delivery again!

Makes 8 servings

Crust:

1 envelope active dry yeast

3 cups sifted all-purpose flour

1½ teaspoons salt

Basic Tomato Sauce:

2 teaspoons olive oil

5 ounces ground chicken or lean chicken sausage (10% or less fat)

½ cup chopped onion

2 garlic cloves, minced

1 cup tomato purée

½ teaspoon dried oregano leaves

½ teaspoon salt

¼ teaspoon black pepper

Topping:

1 or more Special Pizza Additions (recipes follow)

3 ounces shredded or grated cheese (see note above)

1. To prepare crust, in small bowl, sprinkle yeast over ¾ cup + 2 tablespoons warm water (105–115° F); let stand 10 minutes.
2. Set aside 1 tablespoon flour. In food processor, combine remaining flour, the salt and yeast mixture; process 1 minute.
3. Spray large bowl with nonstick cooking spray; place dough in bowl. Cover bowl loosely with plastic wrap; let dough rise in warm, draft-free place until doubled in volume, about 2 hours.
4. Sprinkle work surface with reserved 1 tablespoon flour. Punch down dough; place on prepared work surface. Pat dough into a 12" circle.
5. Spray a 12" pizza pan with nonstick cooking spray. Transfer dough to pan; shape edge to form rim.
6. To prepare sauce, in medium saucepan, heat oil; add chicken and onion. Cook over medium heat, stirring to break up meat, until onion is golden brown and chicken is no longer pink. Add garlic; cook, stirring constantly, 30 seconds longer. Add tomato purée, oregano, salt and pepper; reduce heat to low. Simmer, stirring occasionally, 15 minutes, until flavors are blended.

7. Adjust oven racks so as to divide oven into thirds; preheat oven to 450° F.
8. Spread crust evenly with sauce to within ½" of edge. Arrange Special Pizza Additions over sauce; bake in lower third of oven 10–15 minutes, until bottom is browned. Sprinkle with cheese; bake 10–15 minutes longer, until crust is golden brown and topping is hot.

Each serving (not including Special Pizza Additions) provides: ¼ Fat; ¾ Vegetable; 1 Protein; 2 Breads

Per serving with ground chicken: 249 Calories; 11 g Protein; 6 g Fat; 38 g Carbohydrate; 91 mg Calcium; 767 mg Sodium; 24 mg Cholesterol; 2 g Dietary Fiber

Per serving with chicken sausage: 247 Calories; 11 g Protein; 5 g Fat; 38 g Carbohydrate; 92 mg Calcium; 850 mg Sodium; 20 mg Cholesterol; 2 g Dietary Fiber

SPECIAL PIZZA ADDITIONS

Choose one or more of these additions to make your pizza even more exciting!

Makes 8 servings each

- Slice 2 cups fresh vegetables, such as mushrooms, onions, bell peppers or zucchini, alone or in any combination. Sauté vegetables in medium non-stick skillet in 1 teaspoon olive oil over medium heat, stirring constantly, until soft.

Each serving provides: ½ Vegetable; 5 Optional Calories

Per serving: 13 Calories; 0 g Protein; 1 g Fat; 2 g Carbohydrate; 4 mg Calcium; 1 mg Sodium; 0 mg Cholesterol; 0 g Dietary Fiber

- Wash and drain 4 cups spinach leaves thoroughly; shred. In medium non-stick skillet, sauté shredded spinach in 1 teaspoon olive oil over medium-high heat, 15 seconds, just until wilted.

Each serving provides: 1 Vegetable; 5 Optional Calories

Per serving: 11 Calories; 1 g Protein; 1 g Fat; 1 g Carbohydrate; 28 mg Calcium; 22 mg Sodium; 0 mg Cholesterol; 1 g Dietary Fiber

- Slice or chop 6 large or 10 small green or black olives.

Each serving provides: 5 Optional Calories

Per serving of green olives: 4 Calories; 0 g Protein; 1 g Fat; 0 g Carbohydrate; 2 mg Calcium; 85 mg Sodium; 0 mg Cholesterol; 0 g Dietary Fiber

Per serving of black olives: 4 Calories; 0 g Protein; 1 g Fat; 0 g Carbohydrate; 3 mg Calcium; 31 mg Sodium; 0 mg Cholesterol; 0 g Dietary Fiber

- Sprinkle pizza with crushed red pepper flakes, chopped fresh basil leaves, dried thyme leaves or dried oregano leaves to taste, alone or in any combination.
- Variation: White Pizza—Omit Basic Tomato Sauce and Special Pizza Additions. In small bowl, combine 1 cup part-skim ricotta cheese, the shredded or grated cheese, and 4 ounces crumbled cooked ground chicken or lean chicken sausage (10% or less fat). Spread on unbaked crust to within ½" of edge; bake in lower third of oven 20–30 minutes, until crust is golden brown and topping is hot.

Each serving provides: 1½ Proteins; 2 Breads

Per serving with ground chicken: 263 Calories; 14 g Protein; 7 g Fat; 35 g Carbohydrate; 164 mg Calcium; 544 mg Sodium; 33 mg Cholesterol; 1 g Dietary Fiber

Per serving with chicken sausage: 261 Calories; 14 g Protein; 7 g Fat; 35 g Carbohydrate; 165 mg Calcium; 626 mg Sodium; 30 mg Cholesterol; 1 g Dietary Fiber

CHICKEN REUBEN

Makes 4 servings

Russian Dressing:

½ cup fat-free mayonnaise-style dressing (12 calories per tablespoon)

2 tablespoons ketchup

1½ teaspoons drained prepared horseradish

½ teaspoon grated onion

½ teaspoon Worcestershire sauce

Sandwiches:

4 ounces skinless cooked chicken, sliced

1½ ounces thinly sliced Swiss cheese

¼ cup rinsed drained sauerkraut

8 slices rye bread

1. Preheat broiler. Line large baking sheet with foil.
2. To prepare dressing, in small bowl, combine mayonnaise dressing, ketchup, horseradish, onion and Worcestershire sauce.
3. To prepare sandwiches, place ¼ of the chicken, cheese, sauerkraut and dressing onto each of 4 slices of bread; top each with another slice bread. Broil 8" from heat until golden brown; with spatula, turn to brown other side.

Each serving provides: ¼ Vegetable; 1½ Proteins; 2 Breads; 30 Optional Calories

Per serving: 295 Calories; 17 g Protein; 7 g Fat; 40 g Carbohydrate; 160 mg Calcium; 991 mg Sodium; 35 mg Cholesterol; 5 g Dietary Fiber

CHICKEN-PINEAPPLE KABOBS

For a flavorful and attractive accompaniment, serve these kabobs with rice cooked in chicken broth and mixed with diced colorful bell peppers and raisins, and a salad of cherry tomatoes.

Makes 4 servings

½ cup canned pineapple chunks (no sugar added), drained (reserve 2 tablespoons juice)

2 tablespoons prepared yellow mustard

1 tablespoon + 1 teaspoon firmly packed dark brown sugar

2 teaspoons vegetable oil

¼ teaspoon ground cloves

10 ounces skinless boneless chicken breasts, cut into 16 equal pieces

4 ounces cooked turkey-ham, cut into 12 equal pieces

½ cup Vidalia onion chunks or frozen baby onions, thawed and drained

1. Soak eight 6" wooden skewers in water for 30 minutes.
2. In large bowl, combine pineapple juice, mustard, brown sugar, oil and cloves. Add chicken, turkey-ham, onion and drained pineapple; toss well to coat thoroughly. Refrigerate, covered, 30 minutes.
3. Preheat broiler. Line large baking sheet with foil; spray with nonstick cooking spray.
4. Alternately thread an equal amount of the chicken, turkey-ham, onion and pineapple onto each skewer; reserve any mustard mixture remaining in bowl. Arrange skewers on prepared baking sheet; broil 6–8" from heat 8–10 minutes; turn. Baste with reserved mustard mixture; broil 5–7 minutes longer, until chicken is cooked through.

Each serving (2 kabobs) provides: ½ Fat; ¼ Fruit; ¼ Vegetable; 3 Proteins; 15 Optional Calories

Per serving: 186 Calories; 23 g Protein; 5 g Fat; 12 g Carbohydrate; 32 mg Calcium; 431 mg Sodium; 59 mg Cholesterol; 1 g Dietary Fiber

Soups

Chicken-Barley Soup
Cream of Chicken Soup
Senegalese Soup
Mulligatawny Soup
Velvet Corn Soup
Chicken Gumbo
Spicy Vietnamese Chicken Soup
Walnut Bisque
Pumpkin-Meringue Bisque

CHICKEN–BARLEY SOUP

Nothing is more warming on a frigid winter day than a hearty bowl of piping-hot soup. This one is a meal in itself.

Makes 4 servings

2 teaspoons vegetable oil

1 cup chopped onions

1 cup chopped carrots

½ cup chopped celery

4½ cups low-sodium chicken broth

8 ounces skinless boneless chicken thighs, cut into bite-size pieces

3 ounces uncooked barley

1 small bay leaf

¼ teaspoon dried thyme leaves

¼ teaspoon dried sage leaves

2 cups coarsely chopped mushrooms

½ teaspoon salt

¼ cup minced fresh flat-leaf parsley

¼ teaspoon black pepper

1. In large saucepan, heat oil; add onions, carrots and celery. Cook over medium heat, stirring frequently, 3–4 minutes, until lightly browned. Add broth; bring liquid to a boil. Add chicken, barley, bay leaf, thyme and sage; reduce heat to low. Simmer 1 hour, until chicken is cooked through and barley is tender.
2. Add mushrooms and salt; simmer 15 minutes, until mushrooms are tender. Stir in parsley and pepper; remove and discard bay leaf.

Each serving (1½ cups) provides: ½ Fat; 2¼ Vegetables; 1½ Proteins; 1 Bread; 25 Optional Calories

Per serving: 238 Calories; 18 g Protein; 7 g Fat; 26 g Carbohydrate; 47 mg Calcium; 412 mg Sodium; 47 mg Cholesterol; 6 g Dietary Fiber

CREAM OF CHICKEN SOUP

Make a meal out of this creamy soup, with a salad and homemade muffins, or add a dash of sherry (25 Optional Calories per 1 fluid ounce; 0 g Fat, 0 g Fiber) and serve it as a first course for a dinner party.

Makes 8 servings

2 teaspoons vegetable oil

1 cup minced onions

1 cup minced carrots

½ cup minced celery

½ cup minced white turnip

5 cups low-sodium chicken broth

2 cups evaporated skimmed milk

⅓ cup + 2 teaspoons all-purpose flour

1 small bay leaf

½ teaspoon salt

8 ounces skinless cooked chicken, diced

2 tablespoons minced fresh flat-leaf parsley

¼ teaspoon dried thyme leaves

¼ teaspoon dried marjoram leaves

¼ teaspoon black pepper

⅛ teaspoon dried sage leaves

1. In large saucepan, heat oil; add onions, carrots, celery and turnip. Cook over medium heat until onion is lightly browned. Add 1 cup of the broth; bring liquid to a boil. Reduce heat to low; simmer, covered, until carrots are tender.
2. In medium bowl, with wire whisk, combine remaining 4 cups broth, the milk and flour, blending until flour is dissolved. Strain and add to onion mixture; stir in bay leaf and salt. Bring liquid to a boil over medium heat, stirring constantly; reduce heat to low. Simmer, partially covered, 10 minutes, stirring frequently.
3. Stir chicken, parsley, thyme, marjoram, pepper and sage into broth mixture; simmer 5 minutes. Remove and discard bay leaf.

Each serving (about 1 cup) provides: ½ Milk; ¼ Fat; ¾ Vegetable; 1 Protein; ¼ Bread; 15 Optional Calories

Per serving: 172 Calories; 16 g Protein; 4 g Fat; 17 g Carbohydrate; 208 mg Calcium; 286 mg Sodium; 28 mg Cholesterol; 1 g Dietary Fiber

Senegalese Soup

Makes 4 servings

1 teaspoon peanut oil

2 teaspoons mild or hot curry powder

2 garlic cloves, mashed into a purée

3 cups low-sodium chicken broth

½ cup evaporated skimmed milk

1 tablespoon + 1½ teaspoons all-purpose flour

¼ cup egg substitute

3 tablespoons creamy peanut butter

Chopped chives to garnish

1. In medium saucepan, heat oil; add curry powder. Cook over low heat, stirring constantly, 5 minutes; add garlic. Cook, continuing to stir, 5 minutes longer.
2. In medium bowl, with wire whisk, combine broth, milk and flour, blending until flour is dissolved; strain and add to curry mixture. Cook over medium heat, stirring constantly, until mixture comes to a simmer; reduce heat to low. Simmer 10 minutes, stirring often.
3. In small bowl, with wire whisk, combine egg substitute and peanut butter, blending until mixture is smooth. Continuing to stir with whisk, slowly add about 1 cup of hot broth mixture; return mixture to saucepan. Cook over low heat, stirring constantly, 2 minutes. Serve hot or cold, sprinkled with chives.

Each serving (1 cup) provides: ¼ Milk; 1 Fat; 1 Protein; 25 Optional Calories

Per serving: 152 Calories; 9 g Protein; 9 g Fat; 10 g Carbohydrate; 110 mg Calcium; 154 mg Sodium; 1 mg Cholesterol; 1 g Dietary Fiber

MULLIGATAWNY SOUP

This is a fragrant and hearty soup, perfect for a winter dinner. Add a salad and you've got a meal.

Makes 8 servings

1 tablespoon + 1 teaspoon peanut oil

2 cups chopped onions

1 cup chopped carrots

½ cup chopped celery

2 tablespoons mild or hot curry powder

2 garlic cloves, minced

1 teaspoon ground coriander

5 cups chicken broth

1 bay leaf

4½ ounces dry lentils, rinsed

6 ounces skinless cooked chicken, finely diced

2 cups evaporated skimmed milk

1 tablespoon fresh lime juice

1 teaspoon coconut extract (optional)

4 cups hot cooked long-grain rice

1. In large saucepan, heat oil; add onions, carrots and celery. Cook over medium heat 3–4 minutes, until lightly browned. Add curry powder, garlic and coriander; reduce heat to low. Cook, stirring constantly, 5 minutes.

2. Add broth and bay leaf to onion mixture; bring to a boil over high heat, scraping up browned bits from bottom of saucepan. Add lentils; reduce heat to low. Simmer, partially covered, 45–60 minutes, until lentils are soft.

3. Add chicken and milk to lentil mixture; simmer 5 minutes, until heated through. Stir in lime juice and coconut extract, if using; remove and discard bay leaf.

4. To serve, divide rice evenly among 8 large soup bowls; top with chicken mixture.

Each serving provides: ½ Milk; ½ Fat; 1 Vegetable; 1½ Proteins; 1 Bread; 15 Optional Calories

Per serving: 343 Calories; 21 g Protein; 6 g Fat; 52 g Carbohydrate; 239 mg Calcium; 725 mg Sodium; 21 mg Cholesterol; 4 g Dietary Fiber

VELVET CORN SOUP

A warm bowl of this delicious Chinese soup is just what the doctor ordered for a cold, blustery day.

Makes 4 servings

1 egg white

1 tablespoon cornstarch

1 tablespoon (½ fluid ounce) dry sherry

10 ounces skinless boneless chicken breasts, cut into 1" pieces

6 cups low-sodium chicken broth

⅓ cup minced scallions

1 tablespoon minced pared fresh ginger root

1 tablespoon minced fresh garlic

2 cups canned cream-style corn

2 teaspoons low-sodium soy sauce

½ teaspoon salt

1. In medium bowl, with wire whisk, combine egg white, cornstarch and sherry, blending until cornstarch is dissolved; add chicken, tossing well to coat thoroughly. Refrigerate, covered, 1 hour.
2. In large pot, bring 4 quarts water to a boil over high heat; reduce heat to low. In batches, add chicken, a few pieces at a time, to simmering water; cook 30 seconds, until chicken pieces turn white. With skimmer or slotted spoon, remove chicken from water quickly; set aside to drain.
3. In large saucepan, bring broth to a boil; add scallions, ginger and garlic. Reduce heat to low; simmer 6–7 minutes to blend flavors. Stir in corn, soy sauce and salt; cook 3 minutes longer.
4. Add chicken to broth mixture; cook 4 minutes, until chicken is just cooked through.

Each serving provides: ¼ Vegetable; 2 Proteins; 1 Bread; 45 Optional Calories

Per serving: 242 Calories; 23 g Protein; 4 g Fat; 30 g Carbohydrate; 25 mg Calcium; 846 mg Sodium; 41 mg Cholesterol; 2 g Dietary Fiber

CHICKEN GUMBO

Some like it hot, so pass the hot pepper sauce when you serve this Creole classic. Be sure not to boil the gumbo after adding the filé powder.

Makes 6 servings

2 teaspoons vegetable oil	1 cup sliced okra
1 cup minced onions	½ cup low-sodium chicken broth
½ cup diced celery	½ teaspoon salt
½ cup diced green bell pepper	½ teaspoon dried thyme leaves
13 ounces skinless boneless chicken breast or thigh, finely diced	1 teaspoon filé powder (optional)
2 ounces cooked Virginia ham, finely diced	¼ teaspoon black pepper
2 cups stewed tomatoes	3 cups hot cooked long-grain rice

1. In medium saucepan, heat oil; add onions, celery and green pepper. Cook over medium heat, stirring frequently, 4–5 minutes, until onions are golden brown.
2. Add chicken and ham to onion mixture; cook, stirring frequently, 3 minutes. Add tomatoes, okra, broth, salt and thyme; reduce heat to low. Cook, covered, stirring occasionally, 30 minutes, until chicken is cooked through and flavors are blended. Remove saucepan from heat; stir in filé powder, if using, and black pepper.
3. To serve, divide mixture evenly among 6 bowls; serve with rice.

Each serving provides: ¼ Fat; 1½ Vegetables; 2 Proteins; 1 Bread; 5 Optional Calories

Per serving: 272 Calories; 21 g Protein; 3 g Fat; 39 g Carbohydrate; 74 mg Calcium; 569 mg Sodium; 41 mg Cholesterol; 4 g Dietary Fiber

SPICY VIETNAMESE CHICKEN SOUP

Spicy and tangy, with a hint of sweetness, this dish is easily prepared and warming on a cold winter's night. If you wish, you may spoon in cooked vermicelli for an even more satisfying dish (½ cup vermicelli provides 1 Bread Selection; 0.5 g Fat, 1 g Fiber).

Makes 4 servings

3 tablespoons Asian fish sauce*	1 cup canned crushed tomatoes
1½ teaspoons grated pared fresh ginger root	¼ cup thinly sliced scallions
1 large garlic clove, minced	2 tablespoons thawed frozen concentrated orange juice
10 ounces skinless boneless chicken breasts, cut into 1" pieces	1 tablespoon granulated sugar
5 cups low-sodium chicken broth	8 drops hot pepper sauce, or to taste

1. In medium bowl, combine fish sauce, ginger and garlic; add chicken, tossing well to coat thoroughly. Refrigerate, covered, at least 1 hour or overnight.
2. In large saucepan, bring broth to a boil; reduce heat to low. Add chicken mixture; cook, stirring occasionally, 2 minutes. Stir in tomatoes, scallions, concentrated orange juice and sugar; simmer until chicken is cooked, about 10 minutes. Stir in hot pepper sauce.

Each serving provides: ¼ Fruit; ¾ Vegetable; 2 Proteins; 35 Optional Calories

Per serving: 187 Calories; 22 g Protein; 4 g Fat; 13 g Carbohydrate; 32 mg Calcium; 217 mg sodium (does not include Asian fish sauce—data unavailable); 41 mg Cholesterol; 1 g Dietary Fiber

Asian fish sauce can be purchased in Asian food stores or the Asian food section of some supermarkets.

WALNUT BISQUE

This sophisticated soup is quick to make. It's delicious hot or cold as a first course for your most elegant dinner party.

Makes 4 servings

2 ounces shelled walnuts

2¾ cups low-sodium chicken broth

3 tablespoons all-purpose flour

1 cup evaporated skimmed milk

½ teaspoon salt

⅛ teaspoon black pepper

Pinch nutmeg

2 tablespoons (1 fluid ounce) dry sherry

1. Chop 2 walnuts and set aside for garnish.
2. In medium saucepan, using wire whisk, combine broth and flour, blending until flour is dissolved. Cook over high heat, continuing to whisk, until mixture comes to a boil. Reduce heat to low; add walnuts. Cook, stirring frequently, 15 minutes, until mixture is thickened.
3. With slotted spoon, remove walnuts to blender or food processor. Add ½ cup of the broth mixture; purée until smooth.
4. Pour walnut mixture and milk into remaining broth mixture; stir in salt, pepper and nutmeg. Cook, stirring occasionally, 5 minutes, until well heated. Add sherry; cook 1 minute longer.
5. To serve, divide broth mixture evenly among 4 soup bowls; sprinkle each with one-fourth of the reserved chopped walnuts.

Each serving provides: ½ Milk; 1 Fat; ½ Protein; ¼ Bread; 20 Optional Calories

Per serving: 195 Calories; 9 g Protein; 10 g Fat; 16 g Carbohydrate; 202 mg Calcium; 386 mg Sodium; 3 mg Cholesterol; 1 g Dietary Fiber

Pumpkin–Meringue Bisque

Make this delicate soup with star-shaped meringues for a celebratory dinner.

Makes 4 servings

Meringues:

- 2 cups low-sodium chicken broth
- 3 egg whites
- ¾ ounce grated Parmesan cheese
- ¼ teaspoon paprika (preferably Spanish)
- ⅛ teaspoon black pepper
- ⅛ teaspoon ground red pepper

Bisque:

- 1 teaspoon corn oil
- ½ cup chopped onion
- 1½ cups cooked pumpkin
- ½ cup evaporated skimmed milk
- ½ teaspoon salt
- ¼ teaspoon black pepper
- ¼ teaspoon dried sage leaves
- Pinch nutmeg

1. To prepare meringues, in large skillet over low heat, bring broth just to a simmer.
2. While broth is heating, in medium bowl, with wire whisk or electric mixer, beat egg whites until stiff but not dry. In small bowl, combine Parmesan cheese, paprika, black pepper and ground red pepper; fold into egg whites (mixture will deflate considerably).
3. Drop half of egg-white mixture by teaspoonfuls onto simmering broth, making 4 meringues and being careful not to crowd; simmer, covered, 4 minutes. With slotted spoon, remove meringues to a plate. Repeat with remaining egg-white mixture.* Remove broth from heat; set aside.
4. To prepare bisque, in medium saucepan, heat oil; add onion. Cook over medium-high heat, stirring frequently, 4–5 minutes, until onion is golden brown. Add 1 cup of the reserved broth; reduce heat to low. Simmer, covered, 10 minutes.

5. In blender or food processor, combine onion mixture and pumpkin; purée until smooth, gradually adding remaining broth. Return mixture to saucepan; stir in milk, salt, pepper, sage and nutmeg. Bring mixture just to a boil; reduce heat to low. Simmer, covered, 5 minutes.

6. Divide pumpkin mixture evenly among 4 soup bowls; carefully place 2 meringues onto each portion.

Each serving (1 cup soup with 2 meringues) provides: ¼ Milk; ¼ Fat; 1 Vegetable; ½ Protein; 10 Optional Calories

Per serving: 114 Calories; 9 g Protein; 4 g Fat; 11 g Carbohydrate; 189 mg Calcium; 478 mg Sodium; 5 mg Cholesterol; 0 g Dietary Fiber

*To make star-shaped meringues, spoon egg-white mixture onto simmering broth all at once; simmer, covered, 5 minutes. With 2 spatulas, carefully lift cooked meringue from broth; set on platter. Let cool. Using a 2" star-shaped cookie cutter, cut out 8–12 stars. When ready to serve, place an equal number of stars on each portion of soup; divide any remaining meringue evenly among soup bowls.

4

Salads

Waldorf Chicken
Chicken Salad in Pineapple Boats
Chicken-Nectarine Salad
Almond-Chicken Salad
Chicken Gazpacho Salad
Tabbouleh Chicken
Pesto Pasta Salad with Sun-Dried Tomatoes
Orzo-Chicken Salad
Olive-Chicken Salad
Smoked Chicken Salad with Crispy Tortilla Chips
Thai Chicken Salad
Warm Chicken Salad with Beans, Rice and Corn
Tea-Smoked Chicken Salad

WALDORF CHICKEN

This cool, crunchy salad is a variation of the classic; serve it on a bed of nutty-flavored arugula to complement the walnuts. For a lovely autumn luncheon, serve it with tiny corn muffins.

Makes 4 servings

¼ cup apple cider

6 dried apricot halves, finely diced

¼ teaspoon instant chicken broth and seasoning mix

7 ounces skinless cooked chicken breasts, diced or julienne-cut

1 small Granny Smith apple, cored and diced

1 ounce shelled walnuts, coarsely chopped

½ cup minced celery

¼ cup fat-free mayonnaise-style dressing (12 calories per tablespoon)

⅛ teaspoon black pepper

1. In small saucepan, bring cider to a boil; stir in apricots and broth mix. Let stand 10 minutes.
2. In medium bowl, combine chicken, apple, reserved cider mixture, walnuts, celery, mayonnaise-style dressing and pepper; toss to combine. Refrigerate, covered, 30 minutes; toss again.

Each serving provides: ½ Fat; ½ Fruit; ¼ Vegetable; 2 Proteins; 20 Optional Calories

Per serving: 178 Calories; 17 g Protein; 6 g Fat; 14 g Carbohydrate; 26 mg Calcium; 241 mg Sodium; 42 mg Cholesterol; 2 g Dietary Fiber

CHICKEN SALAD IN PINEAPPLE BOATS

Grenadine syrup gives this salad a delicious flavor and pretty pink color. For a more natural appearance, use honey instead.

Makes 4 servings

⅔ cup pineapple juice

½ cup apple juice

¼ cup orange juice

10 ounces skinless boneless chicken breasts

1 medium pineapple

1 cup strawberries, halved

1 small apple, cored and diced

½ cup orange sections (no sugar added)

1 tablespoon balsamic vinegar

2 teaspoons grenadine syrup or honey

¼ teaspoon ground allspice

1. In medium saucepan, combine pineapple juice, apple juice and orange juice; bring to a boil. Add chicken; reduce heat to low. Simmer, covered, 10–15 minutes, until chicken is cooked through. Remove from heat; set aside to cool.
2. While chicken is cooling, cut pineapple in half lengthwise; remove and discard core. Scoop out pulp, leaving shells intact. Cover shells with plastic wrap; refrigerate until ready to use. Weigh 9 ounces pineapple pulp; reserve remaining pineapple for use at another time.
3. Cut pineapple pulp into chunks. In large bowl, combine pineapple chunks, strawberries, apple and orange sections, tossing lightly.
4. Cut cooled chicken into chunks or strips; add to pineapple mixture. Strain cooking liquid into small saucepan; add vinegar, grenadine syrup and allspice. Bring liquid to a boil; cook until liquid is reduced to about ½ cup.
5. Pour vinegar mixture over chicken mixture; toss well to combine. Refrigerate, covered, at least 1 hour, tossing several times to blend flavors.
6. To serve, fill each pineapple shell with ½ the chicken mixture.

Each serving provides: 2 Fruits; 2 Proteins; 10 Optional Calories

Per serving with grenadine syrup: 196 Calories; 17 g Protein; 1 g Fat; 28 g Carbohydrate; 37 mg Calcium; 49 mg Sodium; 41 mg Cholesterol; 3 g Dietary Fiber

Per serving with honey: 201 Calories; 17 g Protein; 1 g Fat; 31 g Carbohydrate; 38 mg Calcium; 49 mg Sodium; 41 mg Cholesterol; 3 g Dietary Fiber

CHICKEN-NECTARINE SALAD

Makes 4 servings

1 tablespoon + 1 teaspoon reduced-calorie mayonnaise

1 tablespoon + 1 teaspoon chutney

1 tablespoon Dijon-style mustard

1 teaspoon white wine vinegar

½ teaspoon mild or hot curry powder

¼ teaspoon salt

⅛ teaspoon freshly ground black pepper

6 ounces skinless cooked chicken breast, cubed

1½ ounces Jarlsberg cheese, cubed

2 small nectarines, pitted and coarsely chopped

1 cup chopped scallions

2 medium green bell peppers, halved and seeded

2 tablespoons chopped fresh flat-leaf parsley

1. In small bowl, combine mayonnaise, chutney, Dijon mustard, vinegar, curry powder, salt and black pepper.
2. In medium bowl, combine chicken, cheese, nectarines and scallions. Add mayonnaise mixture to chicken mixture, tossing well to coat thoroughly.
3. Spoon ¼ of the chicken mixture into each green pepper half; serve sprinkled with parsley.

Each serving provides: ½ Fat; ½ Fruit; 1½ Vegetables; 2 Proteins; 10 Optional Calories

Per serving: 199 Calories; 16 g Protein; 8 g Fat; 16 g Carbohydrate; 92 mg Calcium; 426 mg Sodium; 46 mg Cholesterol; 2 g Dietary Fiber

Almond-Chicken Salad

Makes 4 servings

1½ cups plain nonfat yogurt

2 tablespoons mango chutney

2 teaspoons low-sodium ketchup

1 teaspoon mild or hot curry powder

8 ounces skinless cooked chicken breast, shredded

2 cups cooked elbow macaroni

1 cup chopped scallions

¼ cup chopped fresh flat-leaf parsley

2 ounces slivered almonds

1. In medium bowl, combine yogurt, chutney, ketchup and curry powder.
2. In large bowl, combine chicken, macaroni, scallions, parsley and almonds. Add yogurt mixture; toss well to coat thoroughly. Refrigerate, covered, until chilled.

Each serving provides: ½ Milk; 1 Fat; ½ Vegetable; 2½ Proteins; 1 Bread; 20 Optional Calories

Per serving: 376 Calories; 28 g Protein; 12 g Fat; 38 g Carbohydrate; 246 mg Calcium; 210 mg Sodium; 52 mg Cholesterol; 3 g Dietary Fiber

Chicken Gazpacho Salad

This gazpacho-flavored chicken salad makes a light hot-weather dish to serve with corn muffins or pita bread.

Makes 4 servings

1 tablespoon + 1 teaspoon olive oil

1 garlic clove, lightly crushed

1 slice firm white bread, diced

¼ cup low-sodium chicken broth

¼ cup tomato juice

10 ounces skinless boneless chicken breasts, cut into 8 equal pieces

1 cup blanched, peeled, seeded and chopped plum tomatoes

1 cup thinly sliced cucumber (if waxed, pare before slicing)

1 cup thinly sliced green bell pepper

1 cup thinly sliced yellow bell pepper

½ cup sliced scallions

¼ cup red wine vinegar

2 tablespoons slivered fresh basil leaves or minced fresh flat-leaf parsley

1 teaspoon dried oregano leaves

½ garlic clove, mashed

½ teaspoon salt

½ teaspoon coarsely ground black pepper

8 lettuce leaves

1. Preheat oven to 350° F.
2. In medium skillet, heat oil; add crushed garlic. Cook, stirring frequently, until garlic is lightly browned; remove and discard garlic. Add bread to skillet; toss until well coated with oil. Transfer bread to large baking sheet; bake 10–15 minutes, until lightly browned. Remove from oven; set aside.
3. In small saucepan, combine chicken broth and tomato juice; bring to a boil over high heat. Add chicken; reduce heat to low. Simmer, covered, 3 minutes; remove from heat. Let stand 10 minutes, until chicken is cooked through.
4. With slotted spoon, transfer chicken to small, deep, nonreactive bowl.* Add tomatoes, cucumber, green and yellow peppers, scallions, vinegar, basil, oregano, mashed garlic, salt, black pepper and ¼ cup of the broth mixture; toss to combine. Refrigerate, covered, 1 hour.
5. To serve, arrange lettuce leaves on serving platter. Top lettuce with chicken mixture; sprinkle with baked bread cubes.

Each serving provides: 1 Fat; 2¾ Vegetables; 2 Proteins; ¼ Bread

Per serving: 176 Calories; 19 g Protein; 6 g Fat; 12 g Carbohydrate; 58 mg
Calcium; 392 mg Sodium; 41 mg Cholesterol; 2 g Dietary Fiber

*When using acidic ingredients such as vinegar, it's best to use bowls made of nonreactive
material, such as stainless steel or glass. Reactive material, such as aluminum, may cause color and
flavor changes in foods.*

TABBOULEH CHICKEN

Serve this hearty chicken salad warm or at room temperature.

Makes 4 servings

2 tablespoons cider vinegar	½ cup chopped scallions
2 tablespoons orange juice	¼ cup chopped fresh flat-leaf parsley
1 tablespoon olive oil	
½ teaspoon Dijon-style mustard	2 garlic cloves, minced
¼ teaspoon salt	8 ounces skinless cooked chicken breast, cubed
2 teaspoons reduced-calorie tub margarine	2 cups cooked bulgur (cracked wheat)
2 small apples, cored and diced	

1. In small bowl, with wire whisk, combine vinegar, orange juice, oil, Dijon
   mustard and salt; set aside.
2. In large nonstick saucepan, melt margarine; add apples, scallions, parsley
   and garlic. Cook, stirring frequently, 4 minutes, until apples are just tender. Add vinegar mixture, chicken and bulgur; cook, stirring frequently,
   2–3 minutes longer, until heated through.

Each serving provides: 1 Fat; ½ Fruit; ¼ Vegetable; 2 Proteins;
1 Bread; 5 Optional Calories

Per serving: 265 Calories; 20 g Protein; 9 g Fat; 28 g Carbohydrate; 40 mg
Calcium; 229 mg Sodium; 50 mg Cholesterol; 2 g Dietary Fiber

Pesto Pasta Salad with Sun-Dried Tomatoes

To bring out its delicious flavor and texture, serve this pasta salad at room temperature.

Makes 4 servings

3 ounces uncooked small pasta shells or fusilli

8 sun-dried tomato halves (not packed in oil), slivered

8 ounces skinless cooked chicken breast, diced or slivered

½ cup tightly packed fresh basil leaves

1 ounce pine nuts (pignolias)

¾ ounce grated Parmesan cheese

2 teaspoons olive oil

2 large garlic cloves

¼ cup low-sodium chicken broth

¼ teaspoon salt

¼ teaspoon black pepper

1. In large pot of boiling water, cook pasta 7–9 minutes, until just tender. Drain and rinse with cold water until tepid. In small bowl, soak tomato halves in boiling water to cover for 10 minutes; drain, discarding liquid.
2. In medium bowl, combine cooked pasta, soaked tomatoes and chicken; set aside.
3. In food processor or blender, combine basil, pine nuts, Parmesan cheese, oil and garlic; process until almost smooth. With food processor on, add broth slowly, processing until mixture is smooth. Add salt and pepper; process just until combined.
4. To serve, pour basil mixture over chicken mixture; toss well to coat thoroughly.

Each serving (1 cup) provides: 1 Fat; 1 Vegetable; 2½ Proteins; 1 Bread

Per serving: 280 Calories; 26 g Protein; 10 g Fat; 23 g Carbohydrate; 146 mg Calcium; 289 mg Sodium; 52 mg Cholesterol; 2 g Dietary Fiber

Orzo-Chicken Salad

Makes 4 servings

10 ounces skinless boneless chicken breasts, cut into strips

¼ cup fat-free French dressing

1 tablespoon + 1 teaspoon olive oil

2 teaspoons Dijon-style mustard

2 teaspoons balsamic vinegar

¼ teaspoon salt

⅛ teaspoon freshly ground black pepper

3 ounces orzo

1 medium tomato, coarsely chopped

1 tablespoon chopped fresh rosemary leaves or 1 teaspoon dried

1 tablespoon chopped fresh oregano leaves or 1 teaspoon dried

1. Place chicken in gallon-size plastic bag; add dressing. Seal bag, squeezing out air; turn to coat chicken. Refrigerate 1 hour, turning bag occasionally.
2. While chicken is marinating, in medium bowl, with wire whisk, combine oil, Dijon mustard, vinegar, salt and pepper.
3. In medium pot of boiling water, cook orzo 6–8 minutes, until tender; drain. Add cooked orzo to oil mixture, mixing well to coat thoroughly; stir in tomato, rosemary and oregano. Set orzo mixture aside.
4. Spray large nonstick skillet with nonstick cooking spray; place over medium heat. Add chicken mixture; cook, stirring occasionally, 5–8 minutes, until chicken is cooked through.
5. Add chicken mixture to orzo mixture, tossing well to coat thoroughly. Refrigerate, covered, until well chilled.

Each serving provides: 1 Fat; ½ Vegetable; 2 Proteins; 1 Bread; 20 Optional Calories

Per serving: 232 Calories; 19 g Protein; 6 g Fat; 23 g Carbohydrate; 24 mg Calcium; 381 mg Sodium; 41 mg Cholesterol; 1 g Dietary Fiber

Olive-Chicken Salad

Makes 4 servings

1 cup low-sodium chicken broth

¼ teaspoon coarsely crushed coriander seed

¼ teaspoon coarsely crushed cumin seed

4 black peppercorns, coarsely crushed

10 ounces skinless boneless chicken breasts

¼ cup plain nonfat yogurt

2 tablespoons fat-free mayonnaise-style dressing (12 calories per tablespoon)

1 tablespoon fresh lemon juice

1½ teaspoons Dijon-style mustard

20 small pitted black and/or green olives, sliced, to garnish

Watercress leaves to garnish

1. In medium saucepan, combine broth, coriander, cumin and peppercorns; bring to a boil over medium heat. Add chicken; reduce heat to low. Simmer, covered, 10 minutes. Remove saucepan from heat; let stand until cool.
2. With slotted spoon, remove chicken to plate, reserving liquid in saucepan. Cover chicken with plastic wrap and refrigerate until chilled.
3. While chicken is chilling, strain broth into small bowl, discarding solids; return liquid to saucepan. Place saucepan over high heat; cook liquid until reduced to about ¼ cup.
4. In small bowl, combine the reduced broth, the yogurt, mayonnaise-style dressing, lemon juice and Dijon mustard; with wire whisk, mix well.
5. Slice chilled chicken on the diagonal into ¼" slices; arrange on serving platter. Spread chicken with yogurt mixture; serve garnished with olives and watercress.

Each serving provides: ½ Fat; 2 Proteins; 20 Optional Calories

Per serving: 120 Calories; 18 g Protein; 3 g Fat; 4 g Carbohydrate; 51 mg Calcium; 345 mg Sodium; 41 mg Cholesterol; 0 g Dietary Fiber

SMOKED CHICKEN SALAD WITH CRISPY TORTILLA CHIPS

You can top this luscious salad with your favorite dressing, but you may find that the wonderful smoky flavor doesn't need any dressing at all!

Makes 4 servings

2 teaspoons vegetable oil

Two 6" flour tortillas, cut into eighths

1 tablespoon + 1 teaspoon grated Parmesan cheese

8 ounces smoked chicken, cubed

2 cups shredded escarole

1 cup blanched cut green beans (1" pieces)

1 cup red bell pepper strips

1 tablespoon rinsed drained capers, chopped

1. Spray large nonstick skillet with nonstick cooking spray; place over medium heat. Add oil; heat. Add tortilla pieces; sprinkle with Parmesan cheese. Cook, turning frequently, 4–5 minutes, until golden brown. Remove tortilla pieces from skillet; set aside.
2. In large serving bowl, combine chicken, escarole, green beans, red pepper strips and capers. Serve with tortilla chips.

Each serving provides: ½ Fat; 2 Vegetables; 2 Proteins; ½ Bread; 10 Optional Calories

Per serving: 189 Calories; 19 g Protein; 8 g Fat; 10 g Carbohydrate; 69 mg Calcium; 691 mg Sodium; 52 mg Cholesterol; 2 g Dietary Fiber

THAI CHICKEN SALAD

Asian fish sauce, a thin, brown sauce made from shrimp or anchovies, is to Thai and Vietnamese cooking what soy sauce is to Chinese and Japanese dishes. Combined here with mint and lime, this salad offers a refreshing, lively taste.

Makes 4 servings

⅓ cup fresh lime juice

2 tablespoons Asian fish sauce*

2 tablespoons ketchup

1½ teaspoons granulated sugar

10 ounces skinless boneless chicken breasts

4 cups torn romaine lettuce

3 ounces spaghetti, cooked, drained and rinsed

1 medium kirby cucumber, peeled and thinly sliced

2 tablespoons finely chopped fresh mint leaves

½ ounce coarsely chopped dry-roasted unsalted peanuts

1. In large salad bowl, with wire whisk, combine lime juice, fish sauce, ketchup and sugar, blending until sugar is dissolved. In medium bowl, combine chicken and 2 tablespoons lime juice mixture, tossing well to coat thoroughly; refrigerate chicken and remaining lime juice mixture, covered, 1 hour or overnight.
2. Preheat broiler.
3. Broil chicken breasts 6" from heat, 3½ minutes on each side, until lightly browned and cooked through. Remove chicken from broiler; set aside to cool slightly.
4. Slice chicken thinly on the diagonal; add to remaining lime juice mixture, tossing well to coat thoroughly. Add lettuce, spaghetti, cucumber and mint; toss to combine. Serve sprinkled with peanuts.

Each serving provides: ¼ Fat; 2½ Vegetables; 2 Proteins; 1 Bread; 20 Optional Calories

Per serving: 230 Calories; 22 g Protein; 4 g Fat; 26 g Carbohydrate; 45 mg Calcium; 144 mg sodium (does not include Asian fish sauce—data unavailable); 41 mg Cholesterol; 2 g Dietary Fiber

Asian fish sauce can be purchased in Asian food stores or the Asian food section of some supermarkets.

Warm Chicken Salad with Beans, Rice and Corn

This colorful salad is quick to fix, especially if you have leftovers on hand. Make it as spicy-hot as you like, then serve it on a bed of crunchy lettuce with ice-cold beer.

Makes 4 servings

- 3 medium red bell peppers, halved and seeded
- 1 medium jalapeño pepper, halved and seeded, or to taste
- 8 ounces skinless cooked chicken breast, diced or julienne-cut
- 1½ cups hot cooked long-grain rice
- 1 cup mild or hot salsa
- 4 ounces drained cooked red kidney beans
- ½ cup cooked whole-kernel corn
- ½ cup sliced scallions
- 2 tablespoons red wine vinegar
- 1 tablespoon minced fresh cilantro
- ½ teaspoon salt
- ½ garlic clove, minced
- ¼ teaspoon dried oregano leaves

1. Preheat broiler. Line large baking sheet with foil; spray with nonstick cooking spray.
2. Place red and jalapeño peppers on prepared baking sheet; broil 4" from heat until charred on all sides. Transfer pepper halves to sealable plastic bag; seal. Let stand 15 minutes. Peel peppers, then rinse. Dice red peppers; mince jalapeño pepper. Transfer to large bowl.
3. Add chicken, rice, salsa, beans, corn, scallions, vinegar, cilantro, salt, garlic and oregano to roasted peppers, tossing well to combine. Let stand 15 minutes; toss again.

Each serving provides: 2 Vegetables; 2 Proteins; 1½ Breads

Per serving: 309 Calories; 23 g Protein; 5 g Fat; 43 g Carbohydrate; 45 mg Calcium; 692 mg Sodium; 50 mg Cholesterol; 3 g Dietary Fiber

TEA-SMOKED CHICKEN SALAD

Tea-smoking foods, a Chinese specialty, imparts a smoky-sweet flavor to the meat, while it remains juicy and tender. This salad combines sweet, smoky and tangy flavors with crunchy and smooth textures for a delightful, visually appealing dish.

Makes 4 servings

½ teaspoon salt

¼ teaspoon crushed Szechuan peppercorns*

⅛ teaspoon granulated sugar

⅛ teaspoon ground ginger

10 ounces skinless boneless chicken thighs

1 medium scallion, quartered

3 slices pared fresh ginger root

2 garlic cloves, crushed

½ cup uncooked, regular long-grain rice

2 tablespoons firmly packed light or dark brown sugar

1 tablespoon + 1½ teaspoons Lapsang Souchong tea leaves*

½ cinnamon stick

Three 3 × ½" strips orange zest†

4 cups torn lettuce leaves

1½ cups drained canned sliced water chestnuts

3 tablespoons low-sodium chicken broth

2 tablespoons fresh lemon juice

1 tablespoon peanut oil

1 medium papaya, pared, seeded and diced

1. In small bowl, combine salt, peppercorns, granulated sugar and ground ginger; rub into chicken. Place scallion, ginger root and garlic on top of chicken; refrigerate, covered, 1 hour.
2. Set a steamer rack or round baking rack into large saucepan; add 1–2" water, being careful that water does not reach top of rack. Spray large heat-resistant plate with nonstick cooking spray (plate should fit into saucepan).
3. Bring water in saucepan to a boil; reduce heat. Place chicken with scallion, ginger root and garlic, along with any accumulated juices, on prepared plate; set plate on rack. Cook chicken over simmering water, covered, 5 minutes, until almost cooked through. Remove chicken and rack from saucepan; discard liquid in saucepan.

4. Spray same rack with nonstick cooking spray; transfer chicken to rack, discarding scallion, ginger root and garlic.
5. Line same saucepan with foil. Sprinkle foil with rice, brown sugar and tea leaves; add cinnamon stick and orange zest. Place saucepan over medium heat; cook until mixture begins to smoke. Set prepared rack into saucepan; cook, covered, 12 minutes, until chicken is cooked through. Remove chicken from saucepan; set aside to cool.
6. While chicken is cooling, in large bowl, combine lettuce, water chestnuts, broth, lemon juice and oil, tossing well to coat thoroughly; divide evenly among 4 plates. Slice cooled chicken; arrange ¼ of the chicken and papaya on each portion of salad.

Each serving provides: ¾ Fat; ½ Fruit; 2 Vegetables; 2 Proteins; ½ Bread

Per serving: 186 Calories; 16 g Protein; 7 g Fat; 17 g Carbohydrate; 68 mg Calcium; 349 mg Sodium; 59 mg Cholesterol; 1 g Dietary Fiber

Szechuan peppercorns and Lapsang Souchong tea leaves can be purchased in Asian food stores or the Asian food section of some supermarkets. If loose tea leaves are not available, use three tea bags and open to release leaves, discarding bag.

†The zest of the orange is the peel without any of the pith (white membrane). To remove zest from orange, use a zester or vegetable peeler; wrap orange in plastic wrap and refrigerate for use at another time.

5

Sautés and Stir-Fries

Chicken with Cider Sauce

This quick sauté with its sweet-sharp sauce makes a great winter meal. Serve it with mashed potatoes and steamed cabbage.

Makes 4 servings

2 teaspoons vegetable oil

Four 6-ounce chicken thighs, skinned

3 ounces lean turkey sausages (10% or less fat), cut into ¼" pieces

1 cup sliced onions

½ cup apple cider

½ cup low-sodium chicken broth

2 teaspoons cider vinegar

2 small Granny Smith apples, cored, pared and sliced

¼ teaspoon dried thyme leaves

¼ teaspoon black pepper

⅛ teaspoon dried sage leaves

1. In large skillet, heat oil; add chicken and sausages. Cook over medium-high heat 3 minutes, until golden brown on all sides. Remove chicken and sausages from skillet; set aside.
2. To same skillet, add onions; cook, stirring frequently, 4–5 minutes, until onions are golden brown. Add cider, broth, vinegar and reserved chicken and sausages; cook, basting chicken with pan juices, 10 minutes, until chicken and sausages are cooked through.
3. Add apples, thyme, pepper and sage; cook, continuing to baste, until apples are just tender.

Each serving provides: ½ Fat; ¾ Fruit; ½ Vegetable; 3 Proteins; 3 Optional Calories

Per serving: 269 Calories; 23 g Protein; 13 g Fat; 16 g Carbohydrate; 25 mg Calcium; 219 mg Sodium; 82 mg Cholesterol; 2 g Dietary Fiber

GINGER-PEACH CHICKEN

When peaches or nectarines are in season, use fresh instead of canned.

Makes 4 servings

1 teaspoon stick margarine or vegetable oil

Four 3-ounce skinless boneless chicken breasts

1 cup drained canned peach slices (no sugar added), diced

½ cup low-sodium chicken broth

⅓ cup peach nectar

2 teaspoons cider vinegar

2 teaspoons minced pared fresh ginger root

1 teaspoon cornstarch, dissolved in 1 tablespoon cold water

1. In medium skillet, heat margarine; add chicken. Cook 2 minutes on each side, until golden brown. Remove chicken from skillet; set aside.
2. To same skillet, add peach slices, broth, nectar, vinegar and ginger root; cook over medium heat 2–3 minutes, scraping up browned bits from bottom of skillet. Reduce heat to low; stir in dissolved cornstarch. Cook, stirring constantly, until mixture is slightly thickened.
3. Return chicken to skillet; cook 5 minutes, basting occasionally with sauce, until chicken is cooked through and well heated.

Each serving provides: ¼ Fat; ¾ Fruit; 2 Proteins; 5 Optional Calories

Per serving: 148 Calories; 20 g Protein; 2 g Fat; 11 g Carbohydrate; 15 mg Calcium; 77 mg Sodium; 49 mg Cholesterol; 0 g Dietary Fiber

CHICKEN SAUTÉ WITH RIESLING

This dish can be prepared in 20 minutes or less. For an elegant meal, serve it with parslied potatoes, a watercress salad and a glass of the Riesling.

Makes 4 servings

1 tablespoon + 1 teaspoon stick margarine

10 ounces skinless boneless chicken breasts, cut into 8 equal pieces

1 cup sliced shallots

1 cup sliced or julienne-cut carrots

½ cup low-sodium chicken broth

¼ cup (2 fluid ounces) dry Riesling wine

2 tablespoons minced fresh flat-leaf parsley

1 teaspoon white wine vinegar

½ teaspoon dried thyme leaves

½ teaspoon dried chervil leaves

¼ teaspoon salt

¼ teaspoon black pepper

½ teaspoon cornstarch, dissolved in 1 tablespoon cold water

1. In large skillet, heat 2 teaspoons of the margarine; add chicken. Cook over medium-high heat 2 minutes on each side, until golden brown. Remove chicken from skillet; set aside.

2. In same skillet, heat remaining 2 teaspoons margarine; add shallots and carrots. Cook, stirring frequently, 4–5 minutes, until shallots are golden brown; stir in broth, wine, parsley, vinegar, thyme, chervil, salt and pepper. Reduce heat to low; cook, stirring occasionally, 5 minutes, until carrots are tender.

3. Stir in dissolved cornstarch; cook until sauce is slightly thickened. Return chicken to skillet; cook, basting with pan juices, 3 minutes, until chicken is cooked through.

Each serving provides: 1 Fat; 1 Vegetable; 2 Proteins; 15 Optional Calories

Per serving: 169 Calories; 18 g Protein; 5 g Fat; 11 g Carbohydrate; 41 mg Calcium; 248 mg Sodium; 41 mg Cholesterol; 1 g Dietary Fiber

Chicken Sauté Bourguignonne

Makes 4 servings

1 tablespoon + 1 teaspoon olive oil

Four 6-ounce chicken thighs, skinned

2 cups quartered mushrooms

1 cup frozen baby onions, thawed and drained

3 slices crisp-cooked turkey bacon (30 calories per slice), crumbled

½ cup minced onion

¼ cup minced carrot

½ cup (4 fluid ounces) dry Burgundy wine

½ cup low-sodium chicken broth

2 teaspoons all-purpose flour

1 teaspoon tomato paste

½ teaspoon dried thyme leaves

½ teaspoon dried marjoram leaves

¼ teaspoon dried rosemary leaves

¼ teaspoon salt

¼ teaspoon black pepper

Pinch mace or nutmeg

1. In large skillet, heat 2 teaspoons of the oil; add chicken. Cook over medium-high heat 2 minutes on each side, until golden brown. Remove chicken from skillet; set aside.
2. In same skillet, heat remaining 2 teaspoons oil; add mushrooms, baby onions, turkey bacon, minced onion and carrot. Cook, stirring frequently, 4–5 minutes, until golden brown.
3. In small bowl, using wire whisk, combine wine, broth, flour and tomato paste, blending until flour is dissolved; strain and add to onion mixture, stirring to combine. Add thyme, marjoram, rosemary, salt, pepper, mace and reserved chicken; stir to combine. Bring liquid to a boil, stirring constantly; reduce heat to low. Simmer, covered, stirring occasionally, 20 minutes, until mixture is thickened. With slotted spoon, transfer chicken and vegetables to serving platter; keep warm.
4. Cook liquid over high heat 2 minutes, until slightly reduced. To serve, pour liquid over chicken and vegetables.

Each serving provides: 1 Fat; 2 Vegetables; 3 Proteins; 55 Optional Calories

Per serving: 308 Calories; 26 g Protein; 16 g Fat; 10 g Carbohydrate; 44 mg Calcium; 377 mg Sodium; 88 mg Cholesterol; 1 g Dietary Fiber

Chicken Sauté Marsala

Marsala is a lovely wine to have on hand; it gives a hint of sweetness and a richness to both meats and desserts. Try it one day on fruit salad and you'll feel like you're eating an elegant treat.

Makes 4 servings

1 tablespoon + 1 teaspoon stick margarine	½ cup (4 fluid ounces) dry Marsala wine
10 ounces skinless boneless chicken breasts, cut into 8 equal pieces	½ cup low-sodium chicken broth
	¼ teaspoon fennel seed
2 cups thinly sliced onions	¼ teaspoon dried sage leaves
2 cups julienne-cut carrots	¼ teaspoon black pepper

1. In large skillet, heat 2 teaspoons of the margarine; add chicken. Cook over medium heat 2 minutes on each side, until golden brown. Remove chicken from skillet; set aside.
2. In same skillet, heat remaining 2 teaspoons margarine; add onions and carrots. Cook, stirring frequently, 4–5 minutes, until onions are golden brown. Stir in wine, broth, fennel seed, sage and pepper. Cook, covered, 3 minutes, until carrots are tender.
3. Return chicken to skillet; cook, basting with pan juices, 3 minutes, until chicken is cooked through. With slotted spoon, transfer chicken and vegetables to serving platter; set aside and keep warm.
4. Continue to cook liquid in skillet until reduced to about ½ cup. Pour over chicken and vegetables.

Each serving provides: 1 Fat; 2 Vegetables; 2 Proteins; 40 Optional Calories

Per serving: 216 Calories; 18 g Protein; 5 g Fat; 16 g Carbohydrate; 45 mg Calcium; 122 mg Sodium; 41 mg Cholesterol; 3 g Dietary Fiber

ESCABÈCHE (SUMMER CHICKEN SAUTÉ)

This Spanish classic, usually made with fish, is a pretty and refreshing chilled summer dish. It must be made at least 24 hours in advance to allow the flavors to blend.

Makes 4 servings

2 teaspoons olive oil

Four 3-ounce skinless boneless chicken breasts

1 cup sliced onions

1 cup sliced red bell pepper

1 cup sliced green bell pepper

1 cup sliced yellow bell pepper

¾ cup white wine vinegar

½ cup sliced carrot

5 garlic cloves, crushed

1 bay leaf

1 teaspoon dried thyme leaves

½ teaspoon crushed black peppercorns

½ teaspoon salt

8 lettuce leaves

Chopped fresh flat-leaf parsley to garnish

1. In medium skillet, heat oil; add chicken. Cook over medium heat 2 minutes on each side, until golden brown and cooked through. Remove from heat; let stand, covered tightly, 10 minutes.
2. Transfer chicken to medium nonreactive bowl,* allowing any accumulated juices to remain in skillet. To juices in skillet, add onions, red, green and yellow peppers, vinegar, carrot, garlic, bay leaf, thyme, peppercorns, salt and ¼ cup water; bring liquid to a boil. Reduce heat to low; simmer, covered, 10–15 minutes, until vegetables are tender-crisp.
3. Pour hot vegetable mixture over chicken; set aside to cool, then refrigerate, covered, 24 hours, tossing ingredients occasionally. Remove and discard bay leaf.
4. To serve, arrange lettuce leaves on serving platter. Top lettuce with chicken mixture; sprinkle with parsley.

Each serving provides: ½ Fat; 2¾ Vegetables; 2 Proteins

Per serving: 171 Calories; 21 g Protein; 4 g Fat; 13 g Carbohydrate; 56 mg Calcium; 338 mg Sodium; 49 mg Cholesterol; 2 g Dietary Fiber

*When using acidic ingredients such as vinegar, it's best to use bowls made of nonreactive material, such as stainless steel or glass. Reactive material, such as aluminum, may cause color and flavor changes in foods.

CHICKEN SEVILLANA

Makes 4 servings

1 teaspoon olive oil

Four 3-ounce skinless boneless chicken breasts

1 cup sliced onions

½ cup low-sodium chicken broth

½ cup orange juice

¼ cup raisins

½ ounce shelled walnuts, coarsely chopped

1 teaspoon aromatic bitters

¼ teaspoon cinnamon

⅛ teaspoon ground cloves

½ teaspoon cornstarch, dissolved in 1 tablespoon cold water

½ cup orange sections (no sugar added)

1. In medium skillet, heat oil; add chicken. Cook 2 minutes on each side, until golden brown. Remove chicken from skillet; set aside.
2. To same skillet, add onions; cook, stirring frequently, 4–5 minutes, until golden brown. Add broth, orange juice, raisins, walnuts, aromatic bitters, cinnamon and cloves; bring to a boil. Cook until mixture is reduced by about a third.
3. Return chicken to skillet; reduce heat to low. Simmer, basting frequently, 5 minutes.
4. Stir dissolved cornstarch into liquid; continue to simmer, stirring constantly, until slightly thickened. Stir in orange sections; cook until heated.

Each serving provides: ½ Fat; 1 Fruit; ½ Vegetable; 2 Proteins; 10 Optional Calories

Per serving: 203 Calories; 21 g Protein; 5 g Fat; 18 g Carbohydrate; 39 mg Calcium; 65 mg Sodium; 49 mg Cholesterol; 2 g Dietary Fiber

HERBED LEMON CHICKEN

Makes 4 servings

10 ounces skinless boneless chicken breasts, cut into ¼" thick slices

1 egg white, beaten

3 tablespoons plain dried bread crumbs

¼ teaspoon dried thyme leaves

¼ teaspoon dried oregano leaves

¼ teaspoon salt

¼ teaspoon black pepper

2 teaspoons unsalted butter*

2 teaspoons peanut oil

½ cup low-sodium chicken broth

2 tablespoons (1 fluid ounce) dry white wine

2 tablespoons fresh lemon juice

1 tablespoon rinsed drained capers

1 tablespoon minced fresh flat-leaf parsley

Lemon slices to garnish

1. In medium bowl, combine chicken and egg white, tossing well to coat thoroughly; set aside.
2. In gallon-size sealable plastic bag, combine bread crumbs, thyme, oregano, salt and pepper; seal bag and shake to blend. Add 1 chicken slice; seal bag and shake to coat. Place coated chicken slice on large plate; repeat, using remaining chicken slices.
3. In large skillet, heat butter and oil; when foam subsides, add coated chicken slices. Cook 1 minute on each side, until golden brown and cooked through. Transfer chicken to serving platter; keep warm.
4. To same skillet, add broth, wine, lemon juice and capers; cook over medium-high heat 2–3 minutes, until reduced to about ½ cup. Stir in parsley; pour mixture over chicken. Serve garnished with lemon slices.

Each serving provides: ½ Fat; 2 Proteins; ¼ Bread; 30 Optional Calories

Per serving: 151 Calories; 18 g Protein; 5 g Fat; 5 g Carbohydrate; 27 mg Calcium; 301 mg Sodium; 46 mg Cholesterol; 0 g Dietary Fiber

*Stick margarine may be substituted for the butter; increase Fat Selection to 1 and reduce Optional Calories to 15.

Per serving with stick margarine: 151 Calories; 18 g Protein; 5 g Fat; 5 g Carbohydrate; 27 mg Calcium; 310 mg Sodium; 43 mg Cholesterol; 0 g Dietary Fiber

TOMATO-HERB CHICKEN

Makes 4 servings

12 sun-dried tomato halves (not packed in oil)

1 tablespoon + 1 teaspoon olive oil

1 pound chicken thighs, skinned

2 cups quartered mushrooms

1 medium green bell pepper, seeded and cut into 1" pieces

4 garlic cloves, minced

1 teaspoon dried thyme leaves

½ teaspoon dried rosemary leaves, crushed

¼ cup low-sodium chicken broth

1 tablespoon red wine vinegar

1. In small bowl, soak tomato halves in boiling water to cover for 2 minutes; drain, reserving liquid. Chop tomato halves; set aside.
2. In large nonstick skillet, heat oil; add chicken. Cook 5–6 minutes on each side, until golden brown and cooked through. Remove chicken from skillet; set aside.
3. In same skillet, combine mushrooms, green pepper, garlic, thyme and rosemary; cook, stirring frequently, 4–5 minutes, until vegetables are tender. Remove vegetables from skillet; set aside.
4. In same skillet, combine broth, ¼ cup of the reserved tomato liquid, the vinegar and reserved chopped tomatoes; bring liquid to a boil. Return chicken and vegetables to skillet; toss to combine. Cook, stirring frequently, 2 minutes, until heated through.

Each serving provides: 1 Fat; 3 Vegetables; 2 Proteins

Per serving: 206 Calories; 17 g Protein; 11 g Fat; 10 g Carbohydrate; 34 mg Calcium; 66 mg Sodium; 54 mg Cholesterol; 3 g Dietary Fiber

CHICKEN SAUTÉ WITH WATERCRESS

Quick, simple and savory, this sauté uses watercress as a hot vegetable. Like spinach, watercress cooks down considerably and imparts a delicate and delicious flavor to the dish.

Makes 4 servings

1 tablespoon + 1 teaspoon peanut oil	8 cups finely chopped stemmed watercress
10 ounces skinless boneless chicken breasts, cut into 8 equal pieces	¼ cup low-sodium beef broth
	2 teaspoons Worcestershire sauce
2 cups thinly sliced onions	¼ teaspoon salt
4 garlic cloves, minced	¼ teaspoon black pepper

1. In large skillet, heat 2 teaspoons of the oil; add chicken. Cook over medium-high heat 2 minutes on each side, until golden brown. Remove chicken from skillet; set aside.
2. In same skillet, heat remaining 2 teaspoons oil; add onions. Cook, stirring frequently, 3–4 minutes, until lightly browned. Add garlic; cook, stirring constantly, 2 minutes longer.
3. Add watercress to onion mixture; cook, tossing constantly, 30 seconds, until wilted. Transfer mixture to serving platter; keep warm.
4. To same skillet, add broth, Worcestershire sauce, salt, pepper and reserved chicken; cook, basting chicken with pan juices, 3 minutes, until chicken is cooked through.
5. Arrange chicken on top of watercress; top with pan juices.

Each serving provides: 1 Fat; 5 Vegetables; 2 Proteins

Per serving: 164 Calories; 19 g Protein; 6 g Fat; 9 g Carbohydrate; 112 mg Calcium; 240 mg Sodium; 41 mg Cholesterol; 3 g Dietary Fiber

SPICY CHICKEN AND SNOW PEAS

If this came in a white carton, you'd swear it was from your favorite Chinese restaurant.

Makes 4 servings

1 tablespoon low-sodium Worcestershire sauce

2 teaspoons Asian sesame oil

2 teaspoons low-sodium soy sauce

1 teaspoon granulated sugar

1 teaspoon cornstarch

1 teaspoon rice wine vinegar

¼ teaspoon crushed red pepper flakes

10 ounces skinless boneless chicken breasts, cubed

2 teaspoons peanut oil

2 tablespoons minced scallions

1 tablespoon chopped pared fresh ginger root

⅛ teaspoon Asian chili paste*

1 cup snow peas (Chinese pea pods), stem ends and strings removed

1 cup drained canned baby corn

1 tablespoon sesame seeds

1 teaspoon hoisin sauce*

1. In medium bowl, combine Worcestershire sauce, 1 tablespoon water, the sesame oil, soy sauce, sugar, cornstarch, vinegar and crushed red pepper, stirring until cornstarch is dissolved. Add chicken, tossing well to coat thoroughly; let stand 10 minutes.

2. In wok or large skillet, heat peanut oil; add scallions, ginger and chili paste. Stir-fry 1 minute. Add chicken mixture; stir-fry 4–5 minutes, until chicken is cooked through. Add snow peas, corn, sesame seeds and hoisin sauce; stir-fry 2–3 minutes longer, until snow peas are tender.

Each serving provides: 1 Fat; ½ Vegetable; 2 Proteins; ½ Bread; 20 Optional Calories

Per serving: 186 Calories; 20 g Protein; 7 g Fat; 11 g Carbohydrate; 49 mg Calcium; 215 mg Sodium; 41 mg Cholesterol; 3 g Dietary Fiber

*Asian chili paste and hoisin sauce can be purchased in Asian food stores or the Asian food section of some supermarkets.

SPICY CHICKEN WITH TANGERINE

When tangerines are in season, peel and squeeze them, then freeze the peel and juice separately to use when preparing this spicy and sweet Chinese dish. Serve it over rice or noodles.

Makes 4 servings

½ teaspoon salt

½ teaspoon crushed Szechuan peppercorns*

½ teaspoon minced fresh hot chili pepper

10 ounces skinless boneless chicken breast, cut into ½" strips

2 teaspoons vegetable oil

2 teaspoons minced fresh or frozen tangerine peel

1 garlic clove, minced

2 cups cooked broccoli florets

¼ cup low-sodium chicken broth

¼ cup tangerine juice

2 tablespoons hoisin sauce*

1 teaspoon cornstarch, dissolved in 1 tablespoon cold water

1. In medium bowl, combine salt, peppercorns and chili pepper; add chicken, tossing well to coat thoroughly.
2. In large nonstick skillet, heat oil; add tangerine peel and garlic. Cook over medium heat, stirring constantly, 30 seconds. Add chicken mixture; cook, stirring frequently, 4 minutes, until chicken is almost cooked through. Stir in broccoli; cook, stirring frequently, 1 minute longer.
3. In small bowl, combine broth, tangerine juice and hoisin sauce; stir into chicken mixture. Stir in dissolved cornstarch; cook, stirring constantly, 1 minute longer, until mixture is slightly thickened and chicken is cooked through.

Each serving provides: ½ Fat; 1 Vegetable; 2 Proteins; 25 Optional Calories

Per serving: 143 Calories; 19 g Protein; 3 g Fat; 9 g Carbohydrate; 46 mg Calcium; 594 mg Sodium; 41 mg Cholesterol; 2 g Dietary Fiber

Szechuan peppercorns and hoisin sauce can be purchased in Asian food stores or the Asian food section of some supermarkets.

STIR-FRIED CHICKEN WITH MUSHROOMS AND ZUCCHINI

Serve this delicious stir-fry with rice or noodles.

Makes 4 servings

½ cup low-sodium chicken broth

2 tablespoons low-sodium soy sauce

2 tablespoons (1 fluid ounce) dry sherry

1 teaspoon Chinese chili sauce*

½ teaspoon granulated sugar

10 ounces skinless boneless chicken breasts or thighs, cut into ½" pieces

1 tablespoon cornstarch

2 teaspoons vegetable or peanut oil

1¼ cups thinly sliced mushrooms

1 medium zucchini, halved lengthwise, then cut into ½" slices

2 garlic cloves, minced

1 teaspoon minced pared fresh ginger root

1. In small bowl, combine broth, soy sauce, sherry, chili sauce and sugar, stirring until sugar is dissolved; set aside.
2. In medium bowl, sprinkle chicken with 1 teaspoon of the cornstarch; toss well to coat thoroughly. In large nonstick skillet, heat oil; add chicken. Cook over medium-high heat, stirring frequently, 2 minutes, until lightly browned. Add mushrooms and zucchini; cook, stirring constantly, 3 minutes. Add garlic and ginger; cook, stirring constantly, 2 minutes longer, until chicken and vegetables are almost cooked through. Stir in reserved broth mixture; bring liquid to a boil. Cook, stirring occasionally, 1 minute.
3. In small bowl, dissolve the remaining 2 teaspoons cornstarch in 2 tablespoons cold water; stir into chicken mixture. Cook 1 minute, until liquid thickens slightly.

Each serving provides: ½ Fat; 1¼ Vegetables; 2 Proteins; 20 Optional Calories

Per serving: 141 Calories; 18 g Protein; 3 g Fat; 7 g Carbohydrate; 19 mg Calcium; 207 mg Sodium; 41 mg Cholesterol; 0 g Dietary Fiber

---

Chinese chili sauce can be found in Asian food stores or in the Asian food section of most supermarkets. If not available, substitute 1 teaspoon ketchup plus a few drops hot pepper sauce or pinch ground red pepper or crushed red pepper flakes.

CHICKEN WITH CASHEWS

Makes 4 servings

2 tablespoons oyster sauce*

1 tablespoon ginger juice†

¾ teaspoon granulated sugar

9 ounces skinless boneless chicken breasts or thighs, cut into ½" pieces

2 teaspoons cornstarch

2 teaspoons peanut or vegetable oil

1 medium yellow bell pepper, seeded and cubed

1 cup snow peas (Chinese pea pods), stem ends and strings removed

2 garlic cloves, minced

1 medium scallion, thinly sliced

1 ounce coarsely chopped unsalted cashews

1. In small bowl, combine oyster sauce, ginger juice, sugar and ½ cup water, stirring until sugar is dissolved; set aside.
2. In medium bowl, sprinkle chicken with 1 teaspoon of the cornstarch; toss well to coat thoroughly. In large nonstick skillet, heat oil; add chicken. Cook over medium-high heat, stirring frequently, 2 minutes, until lightly browned. Add yellow pepper; cook, stirring constantly, 2 minutes.
3. Add snow peas and garlic to chicken mixture; cook, stirring constantly, 2 minutes, until snow peas are tender-crisp. Stir in reserved oyster sauce mixture; cook, stirring occasionally, 1 minute longer.
4. In small bowl, combine remaining 1 teaspoon cornstarch with 1 tablespoon cold water, stirring until cornstarch is dissolved; stir into chicken mixture. Bring mixture to a boil; cook, stirring constantly, 1 minute, until slightly thickened. Serve sprinkled with scallion and cashews.

Each serving provides: 1 Fat; 1 Vegetable; 2 Proteins; 25 Optional Calories

Per serving: 182 Calories; 18 g Protein; 7 g Fat; 13 g Carbohydrate; 37 mg Calcium; 403 mg Sodium; 37 mg Cholesterol; 1 g Dietary Fiber

Oyster sauce, a thick, dark sauce made of oyster extract and salt, imparts a rich flavor to dishes. It can be purchased in Asian food stores or the Asian food section of some supermarkets.

†To make ginger juice, pare a large piece of fresh ginger root. With a fine grater, grate ginger onto a plate; squeeze grated pulp to extract juice. Discard pulp.*

CHICKEN FRIED RICE

Here's a great way to use up leftover cooked rice! The whole family will enjoy this delicately seasoned dish. Serve it with a crisp salad.

Makes 4 servings

2 teaspoons vegetable oil

1 cup sliced thoroughly washed leeks

1 medium carrot, halved lengthwise, thinly sliced

2 garlic cloves, minced

1 teaspoon grated pared fresh ginger root

8 ounces skinless boneless chicken thighs, cut into ½" pieces

2 ounces cooked ham, chopped

4 cups cooked long-grain rice

2 tablespoons rice wine vinegar

1 tablespoon low-sodium soy sauce

1. In large nonstick skillet, heat oil; add leeks and carrot. Cook over high heat, stirring frequently, 2–3 minutes, until vegetables are tender-crisp. Add garlic and ginger; cook, stirring constantly, 30 seconds longer.
2. Add chicken and ham to leek mixture; cook, stirring frequently, 5 minutes, until chicken is cooked through. Add rice; cook, stirring constantly, until heated. Remove from heat; stir in vinegar and soy sauce.

Each serving provides: ½ Fat; 1 Vegetable; 2 Proteins; 2 Breads

Per serving: 404 Calories; 20 g Protein; 6 g Fat; 65 g Carbohydrate; 54 mg Calcium; 336 mg Sodium; 55 mg Cholesterol; 2 g Dietary Fiber

SCALLION CHICKEN AND SOBA NOODLES

Makes 4 servings

2 teaspoons vegetable oil

10 ounces skinless boneless chicken thighs, cut into ½" pieces

1 medium red bell pepper, seeded and diced

1 tablespoon chopped pared fresh ginger root

3 garlic cloves, minced

4 cups stemmed watercress leaves

1½ cups thinly sliced scallions

6 ounces buckwheat soba noodles, cooked and drained*

3 tablespoons (1½ fluid ounces) mirin†

2 tablespoons low-sodium soy sauce

1. In large skillet, heat oil; add chicken. Cook over medium-high heat, stirring frequently, 3 minutes, until chicken is lightly browned.
2. Add red pepper to chicken; cook, stirring frequently, 3 minutes. Stir in ginger and garlic; cook, stirring frequently, 30 seconds longer. Add watercress and scallions; cook, stirring frequently, until watercress is wilted and scallions are tender.
3. Add noodles; cook, tossing constantly, 2 minutes. Stir in mirin and soy sauce; cook until heated through.

Each serving provides: ½ Fat; 3¼ Vegetables; 2 Proteins; 2 Breads; 15 Optional Calories

Per serving: 306 Calories; 22 g Protein; 6 g Fat; 42 g Carbohydrate; 97 mg Calcium; 614 mg Sodium; 59 mg Cholesterol; 2 g Dietary Fiber

Buckwheat soba noodles can be purchased at Asian food stores, the Asian food section of some supermarkets and in some health food stores.

†Mirin, a thick, syrupy, sweet Japanese wine, sometimes labeled as sweet cooking rice wine, can be purchased in some liquor stores, Japanese food stores and the Asian food section of some supermarkets.*

SWEET AND SOUR CHICKEN

This classic dish is sweet, yet tangy and chock full of vegetables. Serve it over rice.

Makes 4 servings

3 tablespoons rice wine vinegar

3 tablespoons granulated sugar

3 tablespoons ketchup

1 tablespoon low-sodium soy sauce

1 cup sliced carrots

1 cup broccoli florets

10 ounces skinless boneless chicken breasts, cut into 1" pieces

2 teaspoons cornstarch

2 teaspoons vegetable oil

1 large garlic clove, minced

½ teaspoon grated pared fresh ginger root

1. In medium bowl, combine vinegar, sugar, ketchup, soy sauce and ½ cup water, stirring until sugar is dissolved; set aside.
2. In large pot, cook carrots and broccoli in boiling water to cover, 3 minutes, until tender-crisp; drain and set aside.
3. In medium bowl, sprinkle chicken with 1 teaspoon of the cornstarch; toss well to coat thoroughly. In large nonstick skillet, heat oil; add chicken. Cook over medium-high heat, stirring frequently, 2 minutes, until lightly browned. Add garlic and ginger; cook, stirring constantly, 1 minute longer. Add vinegar mixture; reduce heat to medium. Cook, stirring frequently, 3 minutes, until chicken is cooked through. Add carrots and broccoli; cook, stirring constantly, 1 minute longer.
4. In small bowl, combine remaining 1 teaspoon cornstarch with 1 tablespoon cold water, stirring until cornstarch is dissolved; stir into chicken mixture. Bring mixture to a simmer; cook, stirring constantly, 1 minute, until slightly thickened.

Each serving provides: ½ Fat; 1 Vegetable; 2 Proteins; 50 Optional Calories

Per serving: 179 Calories; 18 g Protein; 3 g Fat; 19 g Carbohydrate; 36 mg Calcium; 298 mg Sodium; 41 mg Cholesterol; 2 g Dietary Fiber

Baked, Roasted and Grilled Chicken

Baked Chicken with Vegetable Stuffing
Barbecued Chicken
Tarragon-Roasted Chicken
Crusty Chili-Spiced "Fried" Chicken
Chicken Bonne Femme
Chicken with Forty Cloves of Garlic
Dijon-Grilled Chicken Cutlets
Mandarin-Stuffed Cornish Hens
Country-Style Cornish Hens
Baked Cornish Game Hens
Butter-Broiled Cornish Hens

BAKED CHICKEN WITH VEGETABLE STUFFING

Makes 8 servings

2 teaspoons stick margarine

2 teaspoons corn oil

1¼ cups diced onions

1 cup diced parsnips

¾ cup diced carrots

¾ cup diced white turnips

¾ cup diced rutabaga (yellow turnip)

½ cup diced celery

2 tablespoons minced fresh flat-leaf parsley

1 teaspoon dried thyme leaves

½ teaspoon dried marjoram leaves

½ teaspoon dried rosemary leaves

½ teaspoon salt

½ teaspoon coarsely ground black pepper

¼ teaspoon dried sage leaves

One 3-pound chicken, skinned

1 cup low-sodium chicken broth

3 tablespoons fresh lemon juice

1. Preheat oven to 350° F. Spray a 13 × 9" baking pan with nonstick cooking spray.

2. In large skillet, heat stick margarine and oil; when foam subsides, add onions, parsnips, carrots, turnips, rutabaga and celery. Cook, stirring frequently, 20 minutes, until vegetables are softened and lightly browned.

3. In small bowl, combine parsley, thyme, marjoram, rosemary, salt, pepper and sage. Stir about ⅓ of the seasoning mixture into vegetable mixture.

4. Stuff chicken with 1½–2 cups of the vegetable mixture; set remaining mixture aside. Truss chicken; sprinkle with the remaining seasoning mixture. Place chicken in prepared baking pan; add broth and 2 tablespoons of the lemon juice to pan. Bake, covered, 1½ hours, basting with pan juices every 15 minutes, until chicken is cooked through and thigh juices run clear when pierced with a fork. Transfer chicken to serving platter; keep warm.

5. Transfer pan juices to small saucepan; add reserved vegetable mixture. Bring liquid to a boil; cook until mixture is reduced by about half. Stir in the remaining 1 tablespoon lemon juice. With slotted spoon, remove vegetables from saucepan and place around chicken on platter; pour reduced liquid over chicken.

Each serving provides: ½ Fat; 1 Vegetable; 2 Proteins; ¼ Bread; 5 Optional Calories

Per serving: 170 Calories; 18 g Protein; 7 g Fat; 9 g Carbohydrate; 44 mg Calcium; 227 mg Sodium; 50 mg Cholesterol; 2 g Dietary Fiber

Barbecued Chicken

This is the delicious recipe pictured on the cover!

Makes 4 servings

½ cup white vinegar

6 garlic cloves, peeled

½ teaspoon freshly ground black pepper

One 2-pound 4-ounces chicken, skinned and cut into 4 equal parts

Barbecue Sauce:

⅓ cup low-sodium ketchup

1 tablespoon firmly packed light brown sugar

1 tablespoon grated onion

2 teaspoons cider vinegar

1 teaspoon Worcestershire sauce

1 teaspoon Dijon mustard

1. To prepare marinade, combine 2 cups water, white vinegar, garlic and pepper in gallon-size sealable plastic bag. Add chicken; seal bag, squeezing out air; turn to coat chicken. Refrigerate at least 2 hours or overnight, turning bag occasionally.
2. Spray grill rack with nonstick cooking spray. Place grill rack 5" from coals. Prepare grill according to manufacturer's directions.
3. To prepare barbecue sauce, in small saucepan, combine ketchup, sugar, onion, cider vinegar, Worcestershire sauce and mustard. Bring to boil; reduce heat to low and simmer 5 minutes. Set aside.
4. Drain and discard marinade; grill chicken 10 minutes. Brush both sides with barbecue sauce and grill 10–15 minutes longer, turning and brushing with remaining sauce, until cooked through. Serve with grilled corn.

Each serving provides: 3 Proteins; 30 Optional Calories

Per serving: 194 Calories; 25 g Protein; 6 g Fat; 8 g Carbohydrate; 249 mg Sodium; 76 mg Cholesterol; 0 g Dietary Fiber

TARRAGON-ROASTED CHICKEN

Makes 8 servings

Chicken:

One 3-pound chicken

2 tablespoons minced shallots

2 tablespoons minced fresh tarragon

2 teaspoons Dijon-style mustard

1 teaspoon cracked black peppercorns

½ teaspoon salt

Sauce:

¼ cup (2 fluid ounces) dry white wine

¼ cup low-sodium chicken broth

3 tablespoons white wine vinegar

2 tablespoons minced shallots

2 tablespoons fat-free mayonnaise-style dressing (12 calories per tablespoon)

1 tablespoon minced fresh tarragon

1. Preheat oven to 325° F. Spray a 2-quart baking dish with nonstick cooking spray.
2. To prepare chicken, loosen skin of chicken carefully; set in prepared baking dish.
3. In small bowl, combine shallots, tarragon, Dijon mustard, peppercorns and salt; spoon ⅔ of mixture under skin; spread remaining mixture inside chicken.
4. Roast chicken 1½ hours, basting every 15 minutes with pan juices, until cooked through and thigh juices run clear when pierced with a fork.
5. Transfer chicken to serving platter; remove and discard skin. Keep chicken warm.
6. To prepare sauce, strain pan juices into a cup; refrigerate until fat congeals on top. Remove and discard fat.* Pour juices into small saucepan; add wine, broth, vinegar and shallots. Bring to a boil over high heat; cook until mixture is reduced by about half. With wire whisk, stir in mayonnaise-style dressing and tarragon. Serve sauce with chicken.

Each serving provides: 2 Proteins; 10 Optional Calories

Per serving: 125 Calories; 17 g Protein; 4 g Fat; 2 g Carbohydrate; 18 mg Calcium; 274 mg Sodium; 50 mg Cholesterol; 0 g Dietary Fiber

*To save time, a degreasing jug with a spout at the bottom can be used to separate the flavorful juices from the fat, without the need to refrigerate. It can be found at specialty housewares stores.

CRUSTY CHILI-SPICED "FRIED" CHICKEN

If you love fried chicken, this baked version will be perfect for you.

Makes 4 servings

2 slices whole-wheat bread, cubed

1 tablespoon grated lime peel

2 teaspoons mild or hot chili powder

1 teaspoon garlic powder

½ teaspoon ground coriander

1 egg white

Four 3-ounce skinless boneless chicken breasts

2 teaspoons olive oil

1. Spray large baking sheet with nonstick cooking spray.
2. In food processor, combine bread cubes, lime peel, chili powder, garlic powder and coriander; process until crumbly.
3. Place bread crumb mixture on large sheet of wax paper. In shallow bowl, beat egg white lightly. One at a time, dip each chicken breast into egg white, then bread crumb mixture, turning to coat both sides. Place chicken on prepared baking sheet; refrigerate 30 minutes.
4. Preheat oven to 350° F.
5. Drizzle each chicken breast with ½ teaspoon olive oil; bake 15–20 minutes, until chicken is cooked through and coating is crisp.

Each serving provides: ½ Fat; 2 Proteins; ½ Bread; 5 Optional Calories

Per serving: 162 Calories; 22 g Protein; 4 g Fat; 8 g Carbohydrate; 27 mg Calcium; 157 mg Sodium; 49 mg Cholesterol; 1 g Dietary Fiber

CHICKEN BONNE FEMME

Makes 8 servings

One 3-pound chicken, skinned

½ medium onion

1 celery stalk, halved

3 fresh flat-leaf parsley sprigs

1 bay leaf

3 slices crisp-cooked turkey bacon (30 calories per slice), crumbled

½ teaspoon dried thyme leaves

½ cup (4 fluid ounces) dry white wine

¼ cup low-sodium chicken broth

1 pound 14 ounces whole small red potatoes

2 tablespoons minced fresh flat-leaf parsley

½ teaspoon salt

½ teaspoon coarsely ground black pepper

1. Preheat oven to 350° F. Spray a 13 × 9" baking pan with nonstick cooking spray.
2. Stuff chicken with onion, celery, parsley sprigs and bay leaf; place in prepared baking pan. Sprinkle chicken with bacon and thyme; pour wine and broth into pan. Bake, tightly covered, 30 minutes. Leave oven on.
3. Surround chicken with potatoes, turning to coat with pan juices. Bake, tightly covered, 1 hour and 15 minutes longer, until potatoes are tender and chicken is cooked through and thigh juices run clear when pierced with a fork.
4. Transfer chicken to serving platter; remove and discard onion, celery, parsley and bay leaf. Let stand 15 minutes.
5. To serve, with slotted spoon, transfer potatoes to platter with chicken; sprinkle with minced parsley, salt and pepper. Serve with pan juices.

Each serving provides: 2 Proteins; ¾ Bread; 25 Optional Calories

Per serving: 219 Calories; 19 g Protein; 5 g Fat; 20 g Carbohydrate; 14 mg Calcium; 266 mg Sodium; 54 mg Cholesterol; 2 g Dietary Fiber

CHICKEN WITH FORTY CLOVES OF GARLIC

Yes, you read right! 4-0! You're sure to love what caramelized garlic and carrots do to this sauce. Pass around crackle-crusted French bread to soak it all up because you won't want to miss a drop.

Makes 8 servings

40 garlic cloves (about 1½ cups)

½ cup sliced carrot

2 tablespoons olive oil

One 3-pound chicken, skinned and cut into 8 pieces

½ teaspoon salt

¼ teaspoon dried thyme leaves

¼ teaspoon dried rosemary leaves

½ cup low-sodium chicken broth

2 tablespoons minced fresh flat-leaf parsley

½ teaspoon coarsely ground black pepper

1. Preheat oven to 350° F. Spray a 13 × 9" baking pan with nonstick cooking spray.
2. In prepared baking pan, combine garlic, carrot and oil, tossing well to coat thoroughly. Bake 20–30 minutes, stirring every 10 minutes, until golden brown (be careful not to burn).
3. Sprinkle chicken with salt, thyme and rosemary; place in baking pan with garlic mixture. Pour broth into pan; bake, tightly covered, 50–60 minutes, until chicken is cooked through and thigh juices run clear when pierced with a fork.
4. Transfer chicken to serving platter. With slotted spoon, transfer garlic and carrot to food processor; purée, slowly adding pan juices, until very smooth. Stir in parsley and pepper; pour over chicken.

Each serving provides: ¾ Fat; 2 Proteins

Per serving: 189 Calories; 19 g Protein; 8 g Fat; 11 g Carbohydrate; 69 mg Calcium; 197 mg Sodium; 50 mg Cholesterol; 0 g Dietary Fiber

Dijon-Grilled Chicken Cutlets

An indoor ridged grill pan brings the fun of outdoor grilling indoors. If you're more of a traditionalist, prepare this flavorful dish outdoors on the grill or indoors under the broiler.

Makes 4 servings

3 tablespoons Dijon-style mustard

2 teaspoons fresh lime juice

1 teaspoon low-sodium teriyaki sauce

1 garlic clove, finely minced

Pinch ground red pepper

Four 3-ounce skinless boneless chicken breasts

1. Spray an indoor ridged grill pan with nonstick cooking spray.
2. In medium bowl, with wire whisk, combine Dijon mustard, lime juice, teriyaki sauce, garlic and ground red pepper. Dip chicken breasts into mixture, one at a time, coating both sides; place on prepared pan.
3. Grill chicken, brushing with any remaining mustard mixture, 4 minutes on each side, until cooked through and juices run clear when pierced with a fork.

Each serving provides: 2 Proteins

Per serving: 112 Calories; 20 g Protein; 2 g Fat; 2 g Carbohydrate; 11 mg Calcium; 414 mg Sodium; 49 mg Cholesterol; 0 g Dietary Fiber

MANDARIN-STUFFED CORNISH HENS

Makes 4 servings

1 large mandarin orange, peeled and sectioned	½ teaspoon salt
	½ teaspoon black pepper
½ cup thinly sliced onion	Two 1-pound Cornish game
⅓ cup balsamic vinegar	hens, skinned*
1 teaspoon dried oregano leaves	

1. Preheat oven to 450° F. Spray a 13 × 9" baking pan with nonstick cooking spray.
2. In small bowl, combine orange sections, onion, vinegar, oregano, salt and pepper; stuff hens with an equal amount of mixture, leaving most of the liquid in bowl. Place stuffed hens in prepared baking pan; surround with any remaining solid stuffing mixture. Baste hens with some of the remaining stuffing liquid; cover pan with foil.
3. Bake, covered, 30–35 minutes, basting several times with remaining stuffing liquid, until hens are cooked through and thigh juices run clear when pierced with a fork. Remove hens and any solid stuffing mixture to serving platter; set aside and keep warm.
4. Drain pan juices and any remaining basting liquid into small saucepan; bring to a boil. Remove from heat; pour over stuffed hens. To serve, cut hens in half.

Each serving provides: ¼ Fruit; ¼ Vegetable; 3 Proteins

Per serving: 189 Calories; 25 g Protein; 7 g Fat; 6 g Carbohydrate; 30 mg Calcium; 348 mg Sodium; 76 mg Cholesterol; 1 g Dietary Fiber

*A 1-pound Cornish game hen will yield about 6 ounces cooked poultry.

COUNTRY-STYLE CORNISH HENS

Makes 4 servings

1 teaspoon black pepper

½ teaspoon dried thyme leaves

½ teaspoon dried sage leaves

½ teaspoon dried marjoram leaves

⅛ teaspoon nutmeg

½ cup skim buttermilk

Two 1-pound Cornish game hens, skinned and quartered*

⅓ cup + 2 teaspoons plain dried bread crumbs

½ teaspoon paprika

¼ teaspoon onion powder

⅛ teaspoon garlic powder

⅛ teaspoon ground red pepper

2 teaspoons stick margarine

¼ cup minced onion

¾ cup low-sodium chicken broth

¾ cup evaporated skimmed milk

1 tablespoon all-purpose flour

1. In medium bowl, combine ½ teaspoon of the black pepper, the thyme, sage, marjoram and ½ of the nutmeg; remove and set aside ½ teaspoon of mixture. To remaining mixture, add buttermilk; stir to combine. Add hens; turn to coat well with mixture. Refrigerate, covered, 30 minutes.
2. Preheat oven to 425° F. Spray a 13 × 9" baking pan with nonstick cooking spray.
3. In gallon-size sealable plastic bag, combine bread crumbs, paprika, onion powder, garlic powder, red pepper, the remaining ½ teaspoon black pepper and the remaining nutmeg; seal bag and shake to blend. Add 1 hen quarter; seal bag and shake to coat. Place hen in prepared baking pan, cut side down. Repeat, using remaining hen quarters. Bake hens 20 minutes.
4. While hens are baking, in small saucepan, heat margarine; add onion. Cook over medium heat, stirring frequently, 2–3 minutes, until softened. Remove saucepan from heat; with wire whisk, blend in broth, milk, flour and reserved seasoning mixture. Return saucepan to medium heat; cook until mixture comes just to a boil. Reduce heat to low; simmer, stirring often, 10 minutes, until thickened and flavors are blended.
5. Remove hens from oven. Reduce oven temperature to 350° F.
6. Pour broth mixture around hen quarters; bake, tightly covered, 20 minutes longer, until hens are cooked through and thigh juices run clear when pierced with a fork.

7. Remove hen quarters to serving platter. With whisk, mix sauce until smooth; pour over hens.

Each serving provides: ½ Milk; ½ Fat; ¼ Vegetable; 3 Proteins; ½ Bread; 10 Optional Calories

Per serving: 291 Calories; 31 g Protein; 10 g Fat; 18 g Carbohydrate; 223 mg Calcium; 281 mg Sodium; 79 mg Cholesterol; 1 g Dietary Fiber

A 1-pound Cornish game hen will yield about 6 ounces cooked poultry.

BAKED CORNISH GAME HENS

Makes 4 servings

½ cup thawed frozen concentrated orange juice

3 tablespoons tamari

2 tablespoons grated pared fresh ginger root

1 tablespoon minced fresh garlic

Two 1-pound Cornish game hens, skinned and quartered*

1. To prepare marinade, in gallon-size sealable plastic bag, combine concentrated orange juice, tamari, ginger and garlic; add hen quarters. Seal bag, squeezing out air; turn to coat hens. Refrigerate at least 2 hours or overnight, turning bag occasionally.

2. Preheat oven to 375° F. Spray large baking sheet with nonstick cooking spray.

3. Drain marinade into small saucepan; bring to a boil. Remove from heat. Place hens on prepared baking sheet; bake 30–40 minutes, brushing with remaining marinade, until hens are cooked through and thigh juices run clear when pierced with a fork.

Each serving provides: 1 Fruit; 3 Proteins

Per serving: 233 Calories; 27 g Protein; 7 g Fat; 15 g Carbohydrate; 31 mg Calcium; 831 mg Sodium; 76 mg Cholesterol; 0 g Dietary Fiber

A 1-pound Cornish game hen will yield about 6 ounces cooked poultry.

BUTTER-BROILED CORNISH HENS

Don't be alarmed by that tablespoon of hot pepper sauce; it mellows while cooking, producing a delicious, only slightly nippy flavor.

Makes 4 servings

Two 1-pound Cornish game hens, halved*

3 tablespoons fresh lemon juice

1 tablespoon hot pepper sauce

2 teaspoons lightly salted butter, melted†

1 teaspoon dried thyme leaves

½ cup low-sodium chicken broth

1. Spray a 13 × 9" baking pan with nonstick cooking spray.
2. Loosen skin of hens carefully; set in prepared baking pan, skin-side up.
3. In small bowl, combine 2 tablespoons of the lemon juice, 2¾ teaspoons of the hot pepper sauce, the butter and thyme; spoon under skin and all over hens. Refrigerate, covered, at least 2 hours or overnight.
4. Preheat broiler.
5. Broil hens 4" from heat, 8–10 minutes on each side, basting occasionally with pan juices, until cooked through and thigh juices run clear when pierced with a fork.
6. While hens are broiling, in small saucepan, combine broth, the remaining 1 tablespoon lemon juice and the remaining ¼ teaspoon hot pepper sauce; bring to a boil over high heat. Cook until mixture is reduced by about a third.
7. To serve, remove and discard skin from hens; top with broth mixture.

Each serving provides: 3 Proteins; 20 Optional Calories

Per serving: 189 Calories; 25 g Protein; 9 g Fat; 1 g Carbohydrate; 21 mg Calcium; 198 mg Sodium; 81 mg Cholesterol; 0 g Dietary Fiber

A 1-pound Cornish game hen will yield about 6 ounces cooked poultry.

†*Stick margarine may be substituted for the butter; add ½ Fat Selection and reduce Optional Calories to 5.*

Per serving with stick margarine: 189 Calories; 25 g Protein; 9 g Fat; 1 g Carbohydrate; 20 mg Calcium; 201 mg Sodium; 76 mg Cholesterol; 0 g Dietary Fiber

7

Stews and Casseroles

Chicken Fricassee

Makes 4 servings

2 teaspoons vegetable oil

Four 6-ounce chicken drumsticks, skinned

1¼ cups diced onions

¾ cup sliced carrots

¼ cup diced celery

3 cups whole button mushrooms

4 garlic cloves, minced

½ cup low-sodium chicken broth

1 teaspoon all-purpose flour

1 large bay leaf

½ teaspoon dried rosemary
leaves, crushed

¼ teaspoon black pepper

½ cup (4 fluid ounces) dry sherry

2 cups hot cooked long-grain
rice or noodles

1. In large skillet, heat oil; add chicken. Cook 2 minutes on each side, until golden brown. Remove chicken from skillet; set aside.
2. To same skillet, add onions, carrots and celery; cook, stirring frequently, 3–4 minutes, until onion is lightly browned. Add mushrooms and garlic; cook, stirring constantly, 2 minutes longer.
3. In small bowl, using wire whisk, combine broth and flour, blending until flour is dissolved. Strain and add to onion mixture, stirring to combine; bring just to a boil. Reduce heat to low; add bay leaf, rosemary, pepper and re-served chicken. Simmer, covered, 10 minutes, stirring occasionally. Add sherry; cook 10 minutes longer. Remove and discard bay leaf. Serve over rice or noodles.

Each serving provides: ½ Fat; 2¾ Vegetables; 3 Proteins; 1 Bread; 30 Optional Calories

Per serving with rice: 399 Calories; 29 g Protein; 8 g Fat; 43 g Carbohydrate; 56 mg Calcium; 110 mg Sodium; 79 mg Cholesterol; 3 g Dietary Fiber

Per serving with noodles: 373 Calories; 30 g Protein; 9 g Fat; 35 g Carbohydrate; 54 mg Calcium; 114 mg Sodium; 105 mg Cholesterol; 4 g Dietary Fiber

BROWN RICE–CHICKEN FRICASSEE

This homey one-dish meal is ideally suited for cooking ahead of time and reheating.

Makes 4 servings

2 teaspoons canola oil	4 ounces uncooked brown rice
Four 4-ounce skinless boneless chicken thighs	12 sun-dried tomato halves (not packed in oil)
1 cup chopped celery	2 teaspoons ground cumin
1 cup thinly sliced carrots	2 teaspoons finely chopped pared fresh ginger root
1 cup chopped onions	
1 cup low-sodium chicken broth	1 cup thawed frozen peas

1. In Dutch oven or large saucepan, heat oil; add chicken. Cook over medium heat 2 minutes on each side, until golden brown. Remove chicken; set aside.
2. To same Dutch oven, add celery, carrots and onions; cook, stirring frequently, 4–5 minutes, until tender. Return chicken to Dutch oven; add 1½ cups water, broth, rice, tomato halves, cumin and ginger; bring liquid to a boil. Reduce heat to low; simmer, covered, 40–45 minutes, until rice is tender and liquid is absorbed.
3. Stir in peas; cook 2 minutes, until heated through.

Each serving provides: ½ Fat; 3 Vegetables; 3 Proteins; 1½ Breads; 5 Optional Calories

Per serving: 356 Calories; 29 g Protein; 9 g Fat; 41 g Carbohydrate; 72 mg Calcium; 202 mg Sodium; 94 mg Cholesterol; 6 g Dietary Fiber

Chicken Tetrazzini

Makes 4 servings

1   teaspoon vegetable oil

2   cups sliced mushrooms

1   cup diced onions

½   cup finely diced celery

1¼ cups low-sodium chicken broth

½   cup (4 fluid ounces) dry white wine

½   cup evaporated skimmed milk

1   tablespoon + 1½ teaspoons all-purpose flour

½   teaspoon dry mustard

¼   teaspoon dried thyme leaves

4½ ounces thin noodles, cooked, drained and rinsed

6   ounces skinless cooked chicken breast, thinly sliced

¾   ounce grated Parmesan cheese

¾   ounce shredded Gruyère or sharp cheddar cheese

1   tablespoon plain dried bread crumbs

Pinch paprika

1. Adjust oven racks to divide oven into thirds; preheat oven to 400° F. Spray a 1-quart baking dish with nonstick cooking spray.
2. In large skillet, heat oil; add mushrooms, onions and celery. Cook over medium heat, stirring frequently, 7 minutes, until vegetables are softened. Add broth and wine; bring to a boil. Reduce heat to low; simmer 5 minutes.
3. In small bowl, using wire whisk, combine milk, flour, dry mustard and thyme, blending until flour is dissolved. Strain and add to vegetable mixture; cook, stirring constantly, 1 minute, until thickened. Simmer, covered, stirring occasionally, 10 minutes.
4. Place noodles in prepared baking dish; top with chicken, then vegetable mixture.
5. In small bowl, combine Parmesan and Gruyère cheeses and bread crumbs; sprinkle evenly over vegetable mixture, then sprinkle with paprika. Bake in upper third of oven 25–30 minutes, until topping is golden brown and mixture is bubbling.

Each serving provides: ¼ Milk; ¼ Fat; 1¾ Vegetables; 2 Proteins; 1½ Breads; 50 Optional Calories

Per serving: 349 Calories; 26 g Protein; 8 g Fat; 36 g Carbohydrate; 261 mg Calcium; 240 mg Sodium; 78 mg Cholesterol; 2 g Dietary Fiber

CHICKEN-MUSHROOM DINNER

Makes 4 servings

1 teaspoon olive oil

2 cups chopped mushrooms

1 cup chopped onions

½ cup chopped red bell pepper

½ cup low-sodium chicken broth

8 ounces skinless cooked chicken, cubed

1 cup cooked brown rice

1 cup cooked wild rice

½ cup frozen green peas

1 teaspoon salt

1½ teaspoons dried marjoram leaves

½ teaspoon dried rosemary or thyme leaves

¾ teaspoon black pepper

1½ cups sliced plum tomatoes

¾ ounce grated Parmesan cheese

1 tablespoon + 1½ teaspoons plain dried bread crumbs

¼ teaspoon paprika (preferably Spanish)

1. Adjust oven racks to divide oven into thirds. Preheat oven to 425° F.
2. In a flameproof 1-quart casserole, heat oil. Add mushrooms, onions and red pepper; cook over medium-high heat, stirring frequently, until all liquid has evaporated and onions are golden brown. Add broth; cook 2–3 minutes, scraping up browned bits from bottom of casserole. Remove from heat; add chicken, brown rice, wild rice, peas, salt, 1 teaspoon of the marjoram, the rosemary and ½ teaspoon of the black pepper; toss to combine. Top chicken mixture with sliced tomatoes.
3. In small bowl, combine Parmesan cheese, bread crumbs, remaining ½ teaspoon marjoram, remaining ¼ teaspoon black pepper and the paprika; sprinkle evenly over tomatoes. Bake in upper third of oven 15–20 minutes, until crumbs are golden brown.

Each serving provides: ¼ Fat; 2½ Vegetables; 2¼ Proteins; 1¼ Breads; 15 Optional Calories

Per serving: 309 Calories; 25 g Protein; 9 g Fat; 34 g Carbohydrate; 123 mg Calcium; 760 mg Sodium; 55 mg Cholesterol; 4 g Dietary Fiber

Chicken and Eggplant Casserole

Makes 6 servings

Two 1-pound eggplants, each cut lengthwise into 6 equal slices

9 ounces ground chicken

3 ounces lean turkey or chicken sausage (10% or less fat), removed from casing

½ cup minced onion

1 egg, beaten

¼ cup raisins, coarsely chopped

20 small pitted black olives, coarsely chopped

¼ teaspoon cinnamon

¼ teaspoon ground coriander

¼ teaspoon black pepper

1 cup tomato sauce

1½ ounces feta cheese, crumbled

1. Preheat broiler. Line 2 large baking sheets with foil; spray with nonstick cooking spray.
2. Place eggplant slices on baking sheets; broil 4" from heat 10 minutes, until golden brown on one side. Remove eggplant from broiler; set aside to cool.
3. Preheat oven to 400° F. Spray an 8" square baking pan with nonstick cooking spray.
4. Spray medium skillet with nonstick cooking spray; add chicken, sausage meat and onion. Cook, stirring to break up meat, until no longer pink and onion is golden brown. Remove from heat; cool slightly.
5. To cooled chicken mixture, add egg, raisins, olives, cinnamon, coriander and pepper; mix well.
6. Place eggplant slices, broiled side down, on work surface. Spoon an equal amount of chicken mixture 2" from wide end of each slice; roll up to enclose filling.
7. Arrange eggplant rolls, seam-side down, in a single layer in prepared baking pan; top with tomato sauce, then sprinkle with cheese. Bake 35–40 minutes, until bubbling.

Each serving (2 eggplant rolls) provides: ¼ Fat; ¼ Fruit; 2¾ Vegetables; 2 Proteins; 10 Optional Calories

Per serving: 205 Calories; 14 g Protein; 9 g Fat; 19 g Carbohydrate; 122 mg Calcium; 517 mg Sodium; 87 mg Cholesterol; 4 g Dietary Fiber

CHICKEN PARISIENNE WITH NOODLES

Is there a more delicious combination than chicken and noodles? You can pre-pare the chicken ahead of time and pop it in the oven while you cook the noodles.

Makes 4 servings

1 tablespoon + 1 teaspoon stick margarine

9 ounces skinless boneless chicken breasts, cut into 8 equal pieces

2½ cups sliced thoroughly washed leeks

One 10-ounce package (1½ cups) frozen artichoke hearts, thawed and well drained

½ cup thinly sliced carrot

1 cup low-sodium chicken broth

½ cup evaporated skimmed milk

½ teaspoon salt

¼ teaspoon black pepper

3 tablespoons plain dried bread crumbs

¾ ounce grated Parmesan cheese

3 ounces curly noodles, cooked and drained

1. Adjust oven racks to divide oven into thirds. Preheat oven to 425° F. Spray an 8" square baking pan with nonstick cooking spray.
2. In medium skillet, heat 2 teaspoons of the margarine; add chicken. Cook over medium-high heat 2 minutes on each side, until golden brown. Transfer chicken to prepared baking pan; set aside.
3. In same skillet, heat remaining 2 teaspoons margarine; add leeks, artichoke hearts and carrot. Cook, stirring frequently, until leeks are lightly browned.
4. Stir in broth, milk, salt and pepper; bring to a boil over high heat. Cook 5 minutes, until carrot is tender. With slotted spoon, transfer vegetables to baking pan with chicken. Continue to cook broth mixture until reduced to about 1 cup, about 5 minutes; pour over chicken and vegetables.
5. Sprinkle mixture with bread crumbs and Parmesan cheese; bake in upper third of oven 15 minutes, until chicken is cooked through, topping is lightly browned and mixture is bubbling. Serve with noodles.

Each serving provides: ¼ Milk; 1 Fat; 2¼ Vegetables; 2 Proteins; 1¼ Breads; 5 Optional Calories

Per serving: 336 Calories; 27 g Protein; 9 g Fat; 39 g Carbohydrate; 250 mg Calcium; 608 mg Sodium; 63 mg Cholesterol; 5 g Dietary Fiber

BAKED CHICKEN PARMESAN

Makes 4 servings

⅓ cup + 2 teaspoons plain dried bread crumbs

½ teaspoon salt

½ teaspoon dried oregano leaves

½ teaspoon dried basil leaves

½ teaspoon black pepper

12 ounces skinless boneless chicken breasts, pounded thin

1 egg white, beaten

1 tablespoon + 1 teaspoon olive oil

2 cups sliced zucchini

½ cup diced onion

2 garlic cloves, minced

1½ cups tomato purée

⅛ teaspoon crushed red pepper flakes

¾ ounce grated Parmesan cheese

1. Preheat oven to 425° F. Spray an 8" square baking pan with nonstick cooking spray.
2. In gallon-size sealable plastic bag, combine bread crumbs and ¼ teaspoon each of the salt, oregano, basil and black pepper; seal bag and shake to blend.
3. Dip one chicken breast into egg white, turning to coat. Add to bag; seal bag and shake to coat. Place coated chicken breast on large plate; repeat, using remaining chicken breasts.
4. In large nonstick skillet, heat oil; add coated chicken breasts. Cook over medium-high heat, 1 minute on each side, until lightly browned; transfer to prepared baking pan. Add zucchini to skillet; cook, stirring constantly, until golden brown. Arrange zucchini around chicken in pan. Add onion to skillet; cook, stirring constantly, until golden brown. Stir in garlic; cook 1 minute longer. Stir in tomato purée and crushed red pepper; bring mixture to a boil. Reduce heat; simmer 20 minutes, stirring occasionally. Stir in the remaining ¼ teaspoon each salt, oregano, basil and black pepper.
5. Pour tomato mixture over chicken and zucchini; sprinkle with cheese. Bake 15 minutes, until mixture is bubbling and chicken is cooked through.

Each serving provides: 1 Fat; 2¾ Vegetables; 2½ Proteins; ½ Bread; 5 Optional Calories

Per serving: 264 Calories; 27 g Protein; 8 g Fat; 22 g Carbohydrate; 135 mg Calcium; 906 mg Sodium; 54 mg Cholesterol; 3 g Dietary Fiber

FENNEL CHICKEN

If you like fennel, or have never tasted it, try this fragrant peppery dish for a wonderful taste sensation. It goes especially well with a chunk of crusty bread and a glass of Soave.

Makes 8 servings

Three 14-ounce fennel bulbs, trimmed and thinly sliced

1 teaspoon salt

One 3-pound chicken, skinned and cut into 8 pieces

1 tablespoon coarsely crushed fennel seed

1 teaspoon cracked black peppercorns

2 teaspoons olive oil

⅓ cup + 2 teaspoons low-sodium chicken broth

1. Preheat oven to 375° F. Spray an 8" square baking pan with nonstick cooking spray.
2. Place fennel in prepared baking pan; sprinkle with ½ teaspoon of the salt. Bake, loosely covered with foil, 10 minutes, until fennel is softened. Leave oven on.
3. Place chicken pieces bone-side down over fennel. In small bowl, combine fennel seed, peppercorns, olive oil and remaining ½ teaspoon salt; spread evenly over chicken. Pour broth into pan; bake, loosely covered with foil, 30–40 minutes, basting several times with pan juices, until chicken is cooked through and thigh juices run clear when pierced with a fork.
4. With slotted spoon, remove chicken and fennel from baking pan; set on platter and keep warm.
5. Strain pan juices into small saucepan. Bring liquid to a boil over high heat; cook until reduced by about a third. To serve, pour liquid over chicken and fennel.

Each serving provides: ¼ Fat; 1 Vegetable; 2 Proteins

Per serving: 127 Calories; 17 g Protein; 6 g Fat; 2 g Carbohydrate; 32 mg Calcium; 121 mg Sodium; 51 mg Cholesterol; 1 g Dietary Fiber

Chicken-Scallop Gratin

Serve these delightful individual casseroles with rice pilaf or hot biscuits, and a big platter of asparagus.

Makes 4 servings

6 ounces skinless cooked chicken breast, cut into bite-size pieces

2 teaspoons stick margarine

½ cup minced onion

¼ cup minced celery

¼ cup minced green bell pepper

½ cup low-sodium chicken broth

¼ teaspoon dried thyme leaves

13 ounces sea scallops, cut into bite-size pieces

½ cup evaporated skimmed milk

1 tablespoon all-purpose flour

¼ cup fat-free mayonnaise-style dressing (12 calories per tablespoon)

1 teaspoon Dijon-style mustard

½ teaspoon salt

¼ teaspoon black pepper

Pinch ground red pepper

3 tablespoons plain dried bread crumbs

¾ ounce grated Parmesan cheese

1 teaspoon paprika (preferably Spanish)

1. Adjust oven racks to divide oven into thirds. Preheat oven to 450° F. Spray 4 individual ramekins with nonstick cooking spray.
2. Divide chicken evenly among prepared ramekins; set aside.
3. In medium saucepan, heat margarine; add onion, celery and green pepper. Cook over medium heat, stirring constantly, 2–3 minutes, until onion is softened. Add broth and thyme; bring to a boil. Add scallops; remove saucepan from heat. Let mixture stand 5 minutes.
4. With slotted spoon, divide scallops evenly among ramekins.
5. In small bowl, using wire whisk, combine milk and flour, blending until flour is dissolved. Strain and add to broth mixture; continuing to whisk, bring to a boil over high heat. Reduce heat to low; simmer 10 minutes, stirring often. Remove saucepan from heat.
6. With whisk, stir mayonnaise-style dressing, Dijon mustard, salt, black pepper and ground red pepper into broth mixture; divide mixture evenly among ramekins.
7. In small bowl, combine bread crumbs, Parmesan cheese and paprika; sprinkle one-fourth of mixture into each ramekin. Bake in upper third of oven 10 minutes, until topping is golden brown and mixture is bubbling.

Each serving provides: ¼ Milk; ½ Fat; ½ Vegetable; 3 Proteins; ¼ Bread; 20 Optional Calories

Per serving: 278 Calories; 35 g Protein; 7 g Fat; 17 g Carbohydrate; 219 mg Calcium; 897 mg Sodium; 72 mg Cholesterol; 1 g Dietary Fiber

CHICKEN WITH CHESTNUTS

Chestnuts and chicken thighs give this country-style stew a rich, gamelike flavor. Save time and effort by using already peeled frozen chestnuts.

Makes 4 servings

1 teaspoon olive oil	¼ cup (2 fluid ounces) dry white wine
10 ounces skinless boneless chicken thighs, cut into chunks	1 tablespoon tomato paste
1 cup diced onions	1 bay leaf
12 small chestnuts, peeled	½ teaspoon salt
1 cup sliced carrots	2 tablespoons minced fresh flat-leaf parsley
½ cup sliced celery	½ teaspoon dried thyme leaves
½ cup low-sodium chicken broth	¼ teaspoon black pepper

1. In medium skillet, heat oil; add chicken. Cook over medium-high heat, stirring frequently, until golden brown on all sides; add onions. Cook, stirring frequently, until onions are golden brown.
2. Add chestnuts, carrots, celery, broth, wine, tomato paste, bay leaf and salt to chicken mixture; bring liquid to a boil, stirring constantly. Reduce heat to low; simmer 30 minutes, until chicken is cooked through and vegetables are tender.
3. Add parsley, thyme and pepper to chicken mixture; simmer 10 minutes longer, until flavors are blended. Remove and discard bay leaf.

Each serving provides: ¼ Fat; 1½ Vegetables; 2 Proteins; ½ Bread; 15 Optional Calories

Per serving: 248 Calories; 17 g Protein; 5 g Fat; 31 g Carbohydrate; 60 mg Calcium; 409 mg Sodium; 59 mg Cholesterol; 2 g Dietary Fiber

CHEESE GRITS WITH CHICKEN

Makes 4 servings

3 ounces uncooked hominy grits

½ teaspoon salt

3 ounces sharp cheddar cheese

1 tablespoon grated Parmesan cheese

⅛ teaspoon ground red pepper, or to taste

2 teaspoons corn oil

8 ounces skinless boneless chicken breast or thigh

2 ounces cooked Virginia ham, diced or julienne-cut

1 cup frozen baby onions, thawed and drained

½ cup sliced green bell pepper

½ cup sliced red or yellow bell pepper

⅓ cup + 2 teaspoons low-sodium chicken broth

¼ cup chili sauce

1. In medium saucepan, bring 2⅓ cups water to a boil over high heat; stir in grits and salt. Reduce heat to low; simmer 15 minutes, stirring constantly (do not scorch). Cool, covered, until lukewarm.

2. Adjust oven racks to divide oven into thirds; preheat oven to 375° F. Spray an 8" square baking dish with nonstick cooking spray.

3. Stir cheddar and Parmesan cheeses and ground red pepper into grits; spoon mixture into prepared pan, spreading evenly. Bake in upper third of oven 25 minutes, until golden brown.

4. While grits are baking, in medium nonstick skillet, heat oil; add chicken and ham. Cook over medium-high heat, stirring frequently, until mixture is lightly browned. Remove mixture from skillet; set aside.

5. To same skillet, add onions and green and red peppers; cook, stirring frequently, 5 minutes, until onions are golden brown. Add reserved chicken mixture, the broth and chili sauce; bring mixture just to a boil. Reduce heat to low; simmer, covered, stirring frequently, 10 minutes, until onions and peppers are tender and chicken is cooked through.

6. To serve, cut baked grits into 8 equal pieces. Divide chicken mixture evenly among 8 plates; serve with grits.

Each serving provides: ½ Fat; 1 Vegetable; 3 Proteins; 1 Bread; 30 Optional Calories

Per serving: 256 Calories; 23 g Protein; 12 g Fat; 14 g Carbohydrate; 204 mg Calcium; 919 mg Sodium; 64 mg Cholesterol; 1 g Dietary Fiber

BRUNSWICK STEW

Makes 8 servings

2 teaspoons corn oil

One 3-pound chicken, skinned and cut into 8 pieces

1 cup sliced onions

1 cup diced green bell pepper

½ cup diced celery

3 cups low-sodium chicken broth

2 cups stewed tomatoes

1 tablespoon + 1 teaspoon all-purpose flour

2 cups cooked green lima beans

2 cups whole-kernel corn

½ teaspoon salt

2 tablespoons minced fresh flat-leaf parsley

1 tablespoon Worcestershire sauce

1 tablespoon cider vinegar

1 teaspoon hot pepper sauce, or to taste

½ teaspoon black pepper

1. In large, deep skillet, heat oil; add chicken. Cook over medium-high heat 2 minutes on each side, until golden brown. Remove chicken from skillet; set aside.
2. To same skillet, add onions, green pepper and celery; cook, stirring frequently, 4–5 minutes, until onions are golden brown. Stir in broth and tomatoes.
3. In small bowl, with wire whisk, combine ¼ cup cold water and the flour, blending until flour is dissolved; strain and add to broth mixture. Bring mixture to a boil over high heat, stirring constantly; reduce heat to low. Add reserved chicken; simmer 30 minutes, stirring occasionally. Add lima beans, corn and salt; cook, stirring occasionally, 20 minutes longer. Stir in parsley, Worcestershire sauce, vinegar, hot pepper sauce and black pepper.

Each serving provides: ¼ Fat; 1¼ Vegetables; 2 Proteins; 1 Bread; 15 Optional Calories

Per serving: 251 Calories; 23 g Protein; 7 g Fat; 26 g Carbohydrate; 55 mg Calcium; 425 mg Sodium; 50 mg Cholesterol; 5 g Dietary Fiber

CHICKEN CHILINDRON

Makes 8 servings

2 teaspoons olive oil

One 3-pound chicken, skinned and cut into 8 pieces

2 cups sliced onions

2 cups thinly sliced red bell peppers

2 ounces cooked Virginia ham, diced

1 tablespoon minced fresh garlic

2 cups canned Italian tomatoes, chopped (reserve juice)

One 10-ounce package (1½ cups) frozen artichoke hearts, thawed and well drained

¾ cup low-sodium chicken broth

½ cup (4 fluid ounces) dry white wine

6 large pitted black olives, coarsely chopped

6 large pimiento-stuffed green olives, sliced

2 tablespoons minced fresh flat-leaf parsley

1 teaspoon paprika (preferably Spanish)

½ teaspoon dried marjoram leaves

½ teaspoon dried thyme leaves

Pinch powdered saffron, dissolved in 1 tablespoon hot water

1. In large skillet, heat oil; add chicken. Cook 2 minutes on each side, until golden brown. Remove chicken from skillet; set aside.
2. To same skillet, add onions and red peppers; cook, stirring frequently, 4–5 minutes, until onion is lightly browned. Add ham and garlic; cook, stirring constantly, 1 minute longer.
3. Add tomatoes with juice, artichoke hearts, broth, wine, black and green olives, parsley, paprika, marjoram, thyme and saffron; bring liquid to a boil. Reduce heat to low; add reserved chicken. Simmer, covered, 15–20 minutes, until chicken is cooked through and thigh juices run clear when pierced with a fork. With slotted spoon, transfer chicken to serving platter; set aside and keep warm.
4. Bring liquid in skillet to a boil over high heat; cook, stirring constantly, until liquid is reduced by about a third. Serve over chicken.

Each serving provides: ½ Fat; 2 Vegetables; 2¼ Proteins; 15 Optional
  Calories

Per serving: 196 Calories; 20 g Protein; 7 g Fat; 12 g Carbohydrate; 52 mg
  Calcium; 315 mg Sodium; 54 mg Cholesterol; 3 g Dietary Fiber

TEXAS CHICKEN

Makes 4 servings

2 teaspoons corn oil	½ teaspoon cumin seed
Four 6-ounce chicken thighs, skinned	⅛ teaspoon cinnamon
	1 cup stewed tomatoes
2 cups diced red, green and yellow bell peppers	¼ cup low-sodium chicken broth
	1 teaspoon dried oregano leaves
1 cup diced onions	½ teaspoon salt
2 medium jalapeño peppers, seeded and minced, or to taste	½ teaspoon black pepper
	Four 5" ears of corn, halved
1 tablespoon minced fresh garlic	

1. In large skillet, heat oil; add chicken. Cook over medium-high heat 2 minutes on each side, until golden brown. Remove chicken from skillet; set aside.
2. To same skillet, add bell peppers, onions and jalapeño peppers; cook, stirring frequently, 3–4 minutes, until onions are lightly browned. Add garlic, cumin and cinnamon; cook, stirring constantly, 1 minute longer.
3. Return chicken to skillet. Add tomatoes, broth, oregano, salt and black pepper; stir to combine. Bring liquid to a boil; reduce heat to low. Add corn; simmer, covered, stirring occasionally, 20 minutes, until chicken is cooked through and flavors are blended.

Each serving provides: ½ Fat; 2½ Vegetables; 3 Proteins; 1 Bread

Per serving: 328 Calories; 27 g Protein; 13 g Fat; 29 g Carbohydrate; 63 mg
  Calcium; 530 mg Sodium; 81 mg Cholesterol; 6 g Dietary Fiber

BASQUE CHICKEN

People will say, *"Prunes?!* You put *prunes* in the chicken?" Ignore them and forge
ahead; this dish is absolutely delicious. Serve it with rice or crusty bread.

Makes 4 servings

2 teaspoons vegetable oil

Four 6-ounce chicken thighs,
skinned

1 cup chopped red bell pepper

½ cup diced onion

2 garlic cloves, minced

1 cup drained canned Italian
tomatoes, chopped

½ cup (4 fluid ounces) dry red
wine

12 large pimiento-stuffed green
olives, chopped

8 large pitted prunes, chopped

½ teaspoon salt

1. In large skillet, heat oil; add chicken. Cook 2 minutes on each side, until
golden brown. Remove chicken from skillet; set aside.
2. To same skillet, add red pepper and onion; cook, stirring frequently, 4–5
minutes, until onion is lightly browned. Add garlic; cook, stirring constantly,
2 minutes longer.
3. Return chicken to skillet. Add tomatoes, wine, olives, prunes and salt; stir
to combine. Bring liquid to a boil; reduce heat to low. Simmer, stirring
occasionally, 20 minutes, until mixture is thickened and flavors are blended.

Each serving provides: 1 Fat; 1 Fruit; 1¼ Vegetables; 3 Proteins;
25 Optional Calories

Per serving: 272 Calories; 24 g Protein; 9 g Fat; 20 g Carbohydrate; 60 mg
Calcium; 813 mg Sodium; 94 mg Cholesterol; 3 g Dietary Fiber

CHICKEN STROGANOFF

A variation on the beef classic, Chicken Stroganoff is creamy, rich and elegant.
Serve it with noodles and a watercress salad.

Makes 4 servings

1 tablespoon + 1 teaspoon vegetable oil

10 ounces skinless boneless chicken breasts, cut into ½" strips

2 cups sliced mushrooms

1 cup sliced onions

1 cup low-sodium chicken broth

2 teaspoons all-purpose flour

3 tablespoons nonfat sour cream

1 teaspoon red wine vinegar

1 teaspoon Dijon-style mustard

¼ teaspoon black pepper

1. In medium skillet, heat 2 teaspoons of the oil; add chicken. Cook over medium-high heat, stirring frequently, until golden brown. Remove chicken from skillet; set aside.
2. In same skillet, heat remaining 2 teaspoons oil; add mushrooms and onions. Cook, stirring often, until all liquid has evaporated and onions are golden brown.
3. In small bowl, with wire whisk, combine broth and flour, blending until flour is dissolved; strain and add to skillet. Stirring constantly, bring liquid to a boil over high heat; reduce heat to low. Simmer 10 minutes, stirring frequently.
4. Stir reserved chicken into broth mixture; simmer 5 minutes. Remove skillet from heat; stir in sour cream, vinegar, Dijon mustard and pepper.

Each serving provides: 1 Fat; 1½ Vegetables; 2 Proteins; 20 Optional Calories

Per serving: 164 Calories; 19 g Protein; 6 g Fat; 7 g Carbohydrate; 32 mg Calcium; 107 mg Sodium; 41 mg Cholesterol; 1 g Dietary Fiber

COUNTRY CAPTAIN

This is an old favorite—a mild, colorful curry with a delicious combination of sweet and spicy flavors.

Makes 4 servings

2 teaspoons peanut oil

8 ounces skinless boneless chicken thighs, cut into chunks

1 cup diced onions

1 cup diced green bell pepper

1 teaspoon mild or hot curry powder, or to taste

2 garlic cloves, crushed

1 cup stewed tomatoes

½ cup diced celery

½ cup low-sodium chicken broth

2 tablespoons raisins

10 small pimiento-stuffed green olives, sliced

1 teaspoon dried oregano leaves

1 small Granny Smith apple, cored and diced

2 cups hot cooked long-grain rice

1. In medium skillet, heat 1 teaspoon of the oil; add chicken. Cook over medium-high heat 2 minutes on each side, until golden brown. Remove chicken from skillet; set aside.
2. To same skillet, add onions and green pepper; cook, stirring frequently, 4–5 minutes, until onions are golden brown. Reduce heat to low; add remaining 1 teaspoon oil and the curry powder. Cook, stirring constantly, 10 minutes. Add garlic; cook, continuing to stir, 2 minutes. Add tomatoes, celery, broth, raisins, olives, oregano and reserved chicken; cook, stirring occasionally, 20 minutes, until mixture thickens slightly and flavors are blended. Add apple; cook, stirring frequently, 5 minutes longer, until apple is just tender.
3. To serve, spoon rice onto serving platter; top with chicken mixture.

Each serving provides: ¾ Fat; ½ Fruit; 1¾ Vegetables; 1½ Proteins; 1 Bread; 5 Optional Calories

Per serving: 307 Calories; 16 g Protein; 6 g Fat; 47 g Carbohydrate; 73 mg Calcium; 411 mg Sodium; 47 mg Cholesterol; 4 g Dietary Fiber

WILD MUSHROOM STEW

Makes 4 servings

1 teaspoon olive oil	¼ cup low-sodium beef broth
13 ounces skinless boneless chicken thighs, cut into chunks	¼ cup low-sodium chicken broth
	¼ cup (2 fluid ounces) dry red wine
2 ounces cooked Virginia ham, diced	1 teaspoon tomato paste
	¼ teaspoon dried rosemary leaves
4 cups sliced Portobello mushrooms (about 2 large mushrooms)	¼ teaspoon black pepper
	1 tablespoon minced fresh flat-leaf parsley
¼ cup diced onion	
2 garlic cloves, minced	

1. In large skillet, heat oil; add chicken. Cook over medium-high heat 2 minutes on each side, until golden brown. Remove chicken from skillet; set aside.
2. To same skillet, add ham, mushrooms and onion; cook, stirring frequently, 4–5 minutes, until onion is golden. Add garlic; cook, stirring constantly, 2 minutes longer.
3. Stir in beef and chicken broths, wine, tomato paste, rosemary and pepper; bring to a boil. Add reserved chicken; cook, stirring occasionally, 3 minutes, until liquid is reduced to about ½ cup. Serve sprinkled with parsley.

Each serving provides: ¼ Fat; 2 Vegetables; 3 Proteins; 15 Optional Calories

Per serving: 179 Calories; 23 g Protein; 6 g Fat; 6 g Carbohydrate; 23 mg Calcium; 269 mg Sodium; 84 mg Cholesterol; 1 g Dietary Fiber

Chicken Marguerite

Makes 8 servings

2 tablespoons olive oil

1 tablespoon minced garlic

¾ teaspoon salt

½ teaspoon cinnamon

½ teaspoon black pepper

One 3-pound chicken, skinned and cut into 8 pieces

1 pound 4 ounces red potatoes, cut into ⅛" thick slices

¼ cup white wine vinegar

1. Preheat oven to 375° F. Spray an 8" square baking pan with nonstick cooking spray.
2. In large bowl, combine oil, garlic, salt, cinnamon and pepper. Add chicken and potatoes; toss well to coat thoroughly.
3. Arrange chicken in a single layer in prepared baking pan; add vinegar, then top evenly with potatoes. Bake 40–50 minutes, until potatoes are tender, chicken is cooked through and thigh juices run clear when pierced with a fork. Serve topped with pan juices.

Each serving provides: ¾ Fat; 2 Proteins; ½ Bread

Per serving: 199 Calories; 18 g Protein; 8 g Fat; 14 g Carbohydrate; 14 mg Calcium; 260 mg Sodium; 50 mg Cholesterol; 1 g Dietary Fiber

Family Classics

Meatballs and Spaghetti
Bride's Chicken
Chicken Loaf with Tomato Sauce
Chicken Hash
Chicken Chili
Chili Toppings
Chicken à la King
Chicken Cordon Bleu en Croute
Chicken Pot Pie
Chicken and Mushroom Quiche

Meatballs and Spaghetti

Makes 8 servings

Meatballs:

15 ounces ground chicken

1 cup minced onions

¼ cup egg substitute

3 tablespoons plain dried bread crumbs

2 teaspoons tomato paste

3 garlic cloves, minced

½ teaspoon salt

½ teaspoon black pepper

¼ teaspoon dried oregano leaves

¼ teaspoon dried basil leaves

¼ teaspoon crushed red pepper flakes

Pinch cinnamon

2 teaspoons olive oil

Sauce:

2 teaspoons olive oil

1½ cups minced onions

½ cup minced carrot

2 ounces chicken liver

2 ounces cooked ham, minced

3 garlic cloves, minced

1 cup low-sodium beef broth

½ cup tomato paste

½ cup (4 fluid ounces) dry red wine

1 bay leaf

½ teaspoon salt

¼ teaspoon black pepper

Spaghetti:

6 ounces spaghetti, cooked and drained

1. To prepare meatballs, in large bowl, combine chicken, onions, egg substitute, bread crumbs, tomato paste, garlic, salt, black pepper, oregano, basil, crushed red pepper and cinnamon; form into 24 equal meatballs.
2. In large skillet, heat oil; add meatballs. Cook over medium heat, turning as needed, until golden brown on all sides. Transfer meatballs to large saucepan; set aside.
3. To prepare sauce, in same skillet, heat oil; add onions and carrot. Cook over medium heat, stirring frequently, 4–5 minutes, until onions are golden brown. Reduce heat to low; add liver, ham and garlic. Cook, stirring constantly, 3 minutes, until liver is no longer pink.
4. Add ½ cup water to liver mixture; cook, stirring up browned particles from bottom of skillet and mashing liver, until mixture turns pasty.

5. In small bowl, with wire whisk, combine broth, tomato paste and wine, blending until smooth; add to liver mixture. Add bay leaf and salt; stir to combine.

6. Add broth mixture to meatballs; place over low heat. Bring liquid to a boil; reduce heat to low. Simmer 30 minutes, stirring occasionally. Add black pepper; stir to combine. Remove and discard bay leaf.

7. To serve, divide hot spaghetti evenly among 8 plates. Top each portion with 3 meatballs and an equal amount of sauce.

Each serving provides: ½ Fat; 1 ¼ Vegetables; 2 Proteins; 1 Bread; 25 Optional Calories

Per serving: 266 Calories; 17 g Protein; 8 g Fat; 28 g Carbohydrate; 57 mg Calcium; 587 mg Sodium; 79 mg Cholesterol; 3 g Dietary Fiber

Bride's Chicken

Makes 4 servings

Four 3-ounce skinless boneless chicken breasts

¼ cup fat-free vinaigrette dressing

½ envelope (four 8-fluid-ounce servings each) onion soup mix (about 2 tablespoons)

2 tablespoons apricot spreadable fruit

1. Preheat oven to 375° F. Spray an 8" square baking pan with nonstick cooking spray.

2. Place chicken breasts in prepared baking pan. In small bowl, combine dressing, soup mix and spreadable fruit; spread over chicken.

3. Bake 20–25 minutes, until chicken is cooked through and juices run clear when pierced with a fork.

Each serving provides: ½ Fruit; ¼ Vegetable; 2 Proteins; 30 Optional Calories

Per serving: 134 Calories; 20 g Protein; 1 g Fat; 9 g Carbohydrate; 14 mg Calcium; 622 mg Sodium; 49 mg Cholesterol; 0 g Dietary Fiber

Chicken Loaf with Tomato Sauce

Makes 4 servings

14 ounces ground chicken

1¼ cups minced onions

¾ cup tomato sauce

½ cup shredded carrot

1 egg, beaten

¼ cup minced green bell pepper

¼ cup minced fresh flat-leaf parsley

⅓ cup + 2 teaspoons plain dried bread crumbs

2 tablespoons Worcestershire sauce

½ teaspoon dried oregano leaves

¼ teaspoon salt

¼ teaspoon black pepper

4 slices crisp-cooked turkey bacon (30 calories per slice), crumbled

¾ cup sliced mushrooms

½ cup low-sodium beef broth

1. Preheat oven to 350° F. Spray a 13 × 9" baking pan or an 8 × 4" loaf pan with nonstick cooking spray.
2. In large bowl, combine chicken, 1 cup of the onions, ¼ cup of the tomato sauce, the carrot, egg, green pepper, parsley, bread crumbs, 1 tablespoon of the Worcestershire sauce, the oregano, salt and black pepper; form into an 8"-long loaf and place on prepared baking pan or pack into prepared loaf pan. Spread with 2 tablespoons of the remaining tomato sauce; sprinkle with bacon. Bake 1 hour.
3. While meatloaf is baking, spray small nonstick skillet with nonstick cooking spray; add remaining ¼ cup onions and the mushrooms. Cook over medium heat, stirring occasionally, until liquid evaporates and onions are golden brown; add broth and the remaining tomato sauce and Worcestershire sauce. Cook over low heat, stirring frequently, 20 minutes, until flavors are blended.
4. Let meatloaf stand 10 minutes; cut into 8 equal slices. Serve with tomato sauce.

Each serving provides: 2 Vegetables; 3 Proteins; ½ Bread; 35 Optional Calories

Per serving: 302 Calories; 25 g Protein; 14 g Fat; 20 g Carbohydrate; 88 mg Calcium; 875 mg Sodium; 145 mg Cholesterol; 3 g Dietary Fiber

CHICKEN HASH

If you'd like, shape the chicken mixture into equal patties and cook until crisp in a skillet sprayed with nonstick cooking spray.

Makes 4 servings

1   teaspoon stick margarine

½   cup minced onion

½   cup evaporated skimmed milk

¼   cup low-sodium chicken broth

1   tablespoon + 1½ teaspoons all-purpose flour

2   tablespoons (1 fluid ounce) dry sherry

1   teaspoon Worcestershire sauce

½   teaspoon salt

¼   teaspoon black pepper

¼   teaspoon hot pepper sauce

6   ounces skinless cooked chicken breasts, finely diced

6   ounces skinless cooked chicken thighs, finely diced

2   ounces cooked pared potato, finely diced

1. Preheat oven to 400° F. Spray 4 individual ramekins or a shallow square 1-quart baking dish with nonstick cooking spray.
2. In medium saucepan, heat margarine; add onion. Cook over low heat, stirring frequently, 2–3 minutes, until softened. In small bowl, with wire whisk, combine milk, broth and flour, blending until flour is dissolved; strain and add to cooked onion. Continuing to stir with whisk, bring liquid to a simmer; cook, stirring often, 10 minutes.
3. Add sherry, Worcestershire sauce, salt, black pepper and hot pepper sauce to milk mixture; stir to combine. Remove saucepan from heat; stir in chicken breasts and thighs and potato.
4. Divide mixture evenly into prepared ramekins or transfer to prepared baking dish; bake 20 minutes, until browned and heated through.

Each serving provides: ¼ Milk; ¼ Fat; ¼ Vegetable; 3 Proteins; ¼ Bread; 10 Optional Calories

Per serving: 245 Calories; 28 g Protein; 8 g Fat; 12 g Carbohydrate; 113 mg Calcium; 417 mg Sodium; 78 mg Cholesterol; 1 g Dietary Fiber

CHICKEN CHILI

You can make this chili mild, fiery or anywhere in between, by using the appropriate type and amount of chili powder.

Makes 8 servings

1 tablespoon + 1 teaspoon corn oil

2 cups chopped onions

1 tablespoon minced garlic

1 tablespoon mild or hot chili powder, or to taste

1 teaspoon ground cumin

½ teaspoon dried oregano leaves

1 pound 4 ounces skinless boneless chicken thighs, ground or finely chopped

1 cup low-sodium beef broth

1 pound drained cooked dry beans, any variety

2 cups tomato purée

1 tablespoon + 1 teaspoon unsweetened cocoa powder

1. In medium skillet, heat 2 teaspoons of the oil; add onions. Cook over medium-high heat, stirring frequently, 4–5 minutes, until golden brown. Reduce heat to low; add garlic, chili powder, cumin and oregano. Cook, stirring constantly, 3 minutes; transfer mixture to large saucepan.
2. In same skillet, heat the remaining 2 teaspoons oil; add chicken. Cook over medium heat, stirring to break up meat, 4–5 minutes, until no longer pink. Add broth, stirring to loosen browned particles from bottom of skillet.
3. Transfer chicken mixture to saucepan with onion mixture; add beans and tomato purée. Bring mixture to a simmer over medium-low heat; cook 30 minutes, stirring occasionally.
4. In small bowl, combine cocoa and 2 tablespoons boiling water, stirring until cocoa is dissolved; stir into chicken mixture. Cook 5 minutes, until flavors are blended.

Each serving (¾ cup) provides: ½ Fat; 1½ Vegetables; 2 Proteins; 1 Bread; 5 Optional Calories

Per serving: 261 Calories; 22 g Protein; 9 g Fat; 24 g Carbohydrate; 50 mg Calcium; 313 mg Sodium; 54 mg Cholesterol; 5 g Dietary Fiber

CHILI TOPPINGS

Chili is terrific with a variety of different toppings. Serve a few toppings in bowls and let your guests add their favorites. Here are a few to try...

Each makes 8 servings

- In medium bowl, combine 1 cup minced onions and ½ cup minced fresh cilantro.

Each serving provides: ¼ Vegetable

Per serving: 8 Calories; 0 g Protein; 0 g Fat; 2 g Carbohydrate; 5 mg Calcium; 1 mg Sodium; 0 mg Cholesterol; 0 g Dietary Fiber

- In medium bowl, combine 1 cup nonfat sour cream and 1 teaspoon vinegar.

Each serving provides: 20 Optional Calories

Per serving: 20 Calories; 2 g Protein; 0 g Fat; 2 g Carbohydrate; 38 mg Calcium; 20 mg Sodium; 0 mg Cholesterol; 0 g Dietary Fiber

- Shred 6 ounces nonfat cheddar cheese into medium bowl.

Each serving provides: ½ Protein

Per serving: 30 Calories; 6 g Protein; 0 g Fat; 1 g Carbohydrate; 150 mg Calcium; 218 mg Sodium; 2 mg Cholesterol; 0 g Dietary Fiber

Chicken à la King

Makes 4 servings

Croutons:

4 ounces firm, crustless white bread, cut into 4 equal slices

2 tablespoons skim milk

1 tablespoon + 1 teaspoon unsalted butter, melted*

Chicken:

2 teaspoons stick margarine

1¼ cups thinly sliced mushrooms

½ cup minced red bell pepper

¼ cup minced onion

½ cup low-sodium chicken broth

½ cup evaporated skimmed milk

1 tablespoon all-purpose flour

8 ounces skinless cooked chicken breasts, diced (½" dice)

1 tablespoon (½ fluid ounce) dry sherry

½ teaspoon salt

¼ teaspoon black pepper

1. Preheat oven to 350° F. Spray large baking sheet with nonstick cooking spray.
2. To prepare croutons, place bread slices on prepared baking sheet. In small bowl, combine milk and butter; brush bread evenly with mixture. Bake 10–15 minutes, until crisp and golden brown. Remove from oven; set aside.
3. To prepare chicken, in medium saucepan, heat margarine; add mushrooms, red pepper and onion. Cook over medium heat 3–4 minutes, until onion is lightly browned.
4. In small bowl, with wire whisk, combine broth, milk and flour, blending until flour is dissolved. Strain and add to mushroom mixture; cook, stirring constantly, until thickened. Reduce heat to low; simmer 10 minutes, stirring frequently.
5. Add chicken, sherry, salt and black pepper to mushroom mixture; stir to combine. Serve with reserved croutons.

Each serving provides: ¼ Milk; ½ Fat; 1 Vegetable; 2 Proteins; 1 Bread; 50 Optional Calories

Per serving: 279 Calories; 24 g Protein; 9 g Fat; 23 g Carbohydrate; 150 mg Calcium; 540 mg Sodium; 60 mg Cholesterol; 1 g Dietary Fiber

Stick margarine may be substituted for the butter; increase Fat Selection to 1½ and reduce Optional Calories to 15.

Per serving with stick margarine: 279 Calories; 24 g Protein; 9 g Fat; 23 g Carbohydrate; 150 mg Calcium; 584 mg Sodium; 50 mg Cholesterol; 1 g Dietary Fiber

CHICKEN CORDON BLEU EN CROUTE

Makes 4 servings

8 slices reduced-calorie white bread	¼ cup Dijon-style mustard
6 ounces skinless cooked chicken breast, thinly sliced	Pinch ground red pepper, or to taste
2 ounces cooked ham, thinly sliced	½ cup egg substitute
1½ ounces thinly sliced Gruyère cheese	¼ cup skim milk
	2 teaspoons unsalted butter*
	2 teaspoons peanut oil

1. Place 4 bread slices on work surface; top each with ¼ of the chicken, ham and cheese.
2. In small bowl, combine Dijon mustard and red pepper. Spread one side of each remaining bread slice with ¼ of the mustard mixture; place mustard-side down onto each portion of cheese, forming 4 sandwiches.
3. In shallow bowl, combine egg substitute and milk. One at a time, dip each sandwich into mixture, turning to coat both sides.
4. In large skillet, heat butter and oil; when foam subsides, add sandwiches carefully. Cook, turning once and pressing gently with spatula, until golden brown on both sides.

Each serving provides: ½ Fat; 3 Proteins; 1 Bread; 25 Optional Calories

Per serving: 303 Calories; 26 g Protein; 12 g Fat; 24 g Carbohydrate; 188 mg Calcium; 944 mg Sodium; 61 mg Cholesterol; 4 g Dietary Fiber

*Stick margarine may be substituted for the butter; increase Fat Selection to 1 and reduce Optional Calories to 10.

Per serving with stick margarine: 303 Calories; 26 g Protein; 12 g Fat; 24 g Carbohydrate; 188 mg Calcium; 966 mg Sodium; 56 mg Cholesterol; 4 g Dietary Fiber

CHICKEN POT PIE

What could be homier than this creamy pot pie with its old-fashioned quilted crust? A great way to use up leftover chicken!

Makes 4 servings

Topping:

- ¾ cup + 1 teaspoon all-purpose flour
- ¾ teaspoon double-acting baking powder
- ¼ teaspoon salt
- ⅛ teaspoon baking soda
- ¼ cup + 1 tablespoon skim buttermilk
- 1 tablespoon stick margarine, melted

Filling:

- 1 teaspoon margarine
- 1 cup diced carrots
- ½ cup minced onion
- ½ cup minced celery
- 1½ cups low-sodium chicken broth
- ½ cup evaporated skimmed milk
- 3 tablespoons all-purpose flour
- 12 ounces skinless cooked chicken, diced
- 1 cup frozen baby onions, thawed and drained
- ½ cup frozen green peas, thawed
- 2 teaspoons fresh lemon juice
- 1 teaspoon prepared mustard
- ½ teaspoon salt
- ¼ teaspoon black pepper
- ¼ teaspoon dried thyme leaves
- ¼ teaspoon dried marjoram leaves

Pinch dried sage leaves

1. Adjust oven racks to divide oven into thirds. Preheat oven to 425° F. Spray large baking sheet and an 8" square baking pan with nonstick cooking spray.
2. To prepare topping, in small bowl, combine ¾ cup of the flour, the baking powder, salt and baking soda; stir in buttermilk and margarine quickly (mixture will be lumpy).
3. Turn dough out onto prepared baking sheet. Sprinkle fingertips with the remaining 1 teaspoon flour; pat dough into a 7½" square. With sharp knife, score dough into 8 squares. Bake in upper third of oven, 10 minutes, until lightly browned but not fully baked through. Remove topping from oven; set aside. Leave oven on.
4. To prepare filling, in medium saucepan, melt margarine; add carrots, minced onion and celery. Cook over medium heat, stirring frequently, 3 minutes, until lightly browned. Add ½ cup of the broth; bring liquid to a boil. Reduce heat to low; simmer until carrots are tender.
5. In small bowl, with wire whisk, combine the remaining 1 cup broth, the milk and flour, blending until flour is dissolved; strain and add to carrot mixture. Stirring constantly, bring mixture to a boil over medium-high heat; reduce heat to low. Simmer 10 minutes, stirring frequently. Stir in chicken, baby onions, peas, lemon juice, mustard, salt, pepper, thyme, marjoram and sage.
6. Transfer chicken mixture to prepared baking pan. Place topping over chicken mixture; bake in upper third of oven 15 minutes, until topping is golden brown and filling is bubbling.

Each serving provides: ¼ Milk; 1 Fat; 1½ Vegetables; 3 Proteins; 1½ Breads; 15 Optional Calories

Per serving: 404 Calories; 34 g Protein; 12 g Fat; 39 g Carbohydrate; 236 mg Calcium; 775 mg Sodium; 78 mg Cholesterol; 3 g Dietary Fiber

CHICKEN AND MUSHROOM QUICHE

This quiche freezes well, so wrap any extra portions in vapor-proof freezer wrap and you'll have an easy, savory lunch on another day.

Makes 6 servings

Crust:

6 ounces frozen phyllo dough, thawed (about 9 sheets)

2 tablespoons reduced-calorie tub margarine, melted

Filling:

3 cups sliced mushrooms

½ cup sliced shallots

2 garlic cloves, minced

3 eggs, lightly beaten

½ cup evaporated skimmed milk

2 teaspoons dried tarragon

6 ounces skinless cooked chicken, diced

1. Preheat oven to 350° F.
2. To prepare crust, brush 1 side of each phyllo sheet with an equal amount of margarine; stack sheets together. Line a 9" quiche dish or pie plate with phyllo stack. With kitchen shears, trim crust flush with edge of dish; crumble trimmings and sprinkle evenly over crust.
3. To prepare filling, spray large nonstick skillet with nonstick cooking spray; place over medium heat. Add mushrooms, shallots and garlic to skillet; cook, stirring occasionally, until mushrooms are tender and mixture is soft but not dry. Spoon mushroom mixture into prepared crust.
4. In medium bowl, combine eggs, milk and tarragon, beating until frothy; stir in chicken. Pour egg mixture over mushroom mixture; bake 25 minutes, until filling is set and golden brown. Let stand 5 minutes before cutting.

Each serving provides: ½ Fat; 1 Vegetable; 1½ Proteins; 1 Bread; 15 Optional Calories

Per serving: 231 Calories; 16 g Protein; 9 g Fat; 22 g Carbohydrate; 97 mg Calcium; 266 mg Sodium; 132 mg Cholesterol; 1 g Dietary Fiber

9

Parties and Entertaining

125

HAZELNUT CHICKEN

This dish is perfect for company! For a festive meal, serve it with wild rice, asparagus and champagne.

Makes 4 servings

14 ounces skinless boneless chicken breasts, cut horizontally into ¼" thick slices

¼ cup egg substitute

¼ cup plain dried bread crumbs

1 ounce ground hazelnuts

½ teaspoon salt

¼ teaspoon black pepper

2 teaspoons unsalted butter*

2 teaspoons corn oil

½ cup low-sodium chicken broth

½ cup evaporated skimmed milk

2 teaspoons cornstarch

1 small Granny Smith apple, cored, pared and sliced

1 tablespoon (½ fluid ounce) hazelnut liqueur

1 tablespoon (½ fluid ounce) dry sherry

1. In medium bowl, combine chicken and egg substitute, tossing well to coat thoroughly; set aside.
2. In gallon-size sealable plastic bag, combine bread crumbs, hazelnuts, salt and pepper; seal bag and shake to blend. Add 1 chicken slice; seal bag and shake to coat. Place coated chicken slice on large plate; repeat, using remaining chicken slices.
3. In large skillet, heat butter and oil; when foam subsides, add coated chicken slices. Cook 1 minute on each side, until golden brown and cooked through. Transfer chicken to serving platter; keep warm.
4. In small saucepan, with wire whisk, combine broth, milk and cornstarch, blending until cornstarch is dissolved; cook over medium-high heat until slightly thickened. Add apple, liqueur and sherry; cook 5 minutes longer.
5. To serve, spoon broth mixture over chicken.

Each serving provides: ¼ Milk; 1½ Fats; ¼ Fruit; 3 Proteins; ¼ Bread; 50 Optional Calories

Per serving: 288 Calories; 29 g Protein; 11 g Fat; 16 g Carbohydrate; 141 mg Calcium; 460 mg Sodium; 64 mg Cholesterol; 1 g Dietary Fiber

*Stick margarine may be substituted for the butter; increase Fat Selection to 2 and reduce Optional Calories to 30.

Per serving with stick margarine: 288 Calories; 29 g Protein; 11 g Fat; 16 g Carbohydrate; 141 mg Calcium; 482 mg Sodium; 59 mg Cholesterol; 1 g Dietary Fiber

CHICKEN AMANDINE

You'll be surprised by how quickly you can prepare this elegant chicken.

Makes 4 servings

2 teaspoons vegetable oil

10 ounces skinless boneless chicken breasts, cut into 12 equal strips

1 ounce slivered almonds

½ cup (4 fluid ounces) dry white wine

½ cup low-sodium chicken broth

1 teaspoon granulated sugar

1 teaspoon cornstarch

1. In medium skillet, heat oil; add chicken. Cook over medium-high heat 2 minutes on each side, until golden brown. Remove chicken from skillet; set aside.
2. To same skillet, add almonds; cook, stirring constantly, until lightly browned. Remove almonds from skillet; set aside.
3. In small bowl, with wire whisk, combine wine, broth, sugar and cornstarch, blending until cornstarch is dissolved. In same skillet, cook wine mixture until slightly thickened and reduced to about ⅔ cup. Return chicken and almonds to skillet; cook 1 minute, basting constantly with wine mixture.

Each serving provides: 1 Fat; 2¼ Proteins; 35 Optional Calories

Per serving: 170 Calories; 18 g Protein; 7 g Fat; 3 g Carbohydrate; 29 mg Calcium; 55 mg Sodium; 41 mg Cholesterol; 1 g Dietary Fiber

WALNUT-STUFFED CHICKEN BREASTS

These festive stuffed breasts are a welcome addition to a party buffet whether served hot or cold.

Makes 4 servings

Three 4-ounce skinless boneless chicken breasts

2 ounces cooked ham, minced

1 ounce shelled walnuts, chopped

2 tablespoons light cream cheese

1 tablespoon plain dried bread crumbs

¼ teaspoon salt

⅛ teaspoon black pepper

Pinch nutmeg

Pinch ground red pepper

1 teaspoon stick margarine

½ cup diced onion

½ cup diced carrot

½ cup apple cider

¼ cup low-sodium chicken broth

1 tablespoon cider vinegar

1. Preheat oven to 350° F.
2. With sharp knife, slit chicken breasts lengthwise ¾ of the way through; spread apart at slit to open. Place each breast, skinned-side down, between 2 sheets of plastic wrap; with meat mallet, pound chicken lightly to an even ¼" thickness and set aside.
3. In small bowl, combine ham, walnuts, cream cheese, bread crumbs, salt, black pepper, nutmeg and ground red pepper; spoon on equal amount of ham mixture onto each flattened chicken breast. Roll up chicken breasts to enclose filling; secure with kitchen string.
4. In medium ovenproof skillet, heat margarine; add chicken rolls. Cook over medium heat, turning as needed, just until surfaces of rolls turn opaque. Add onion and carrot to skillet; cook, stirring occasionally, 2 minutes longer.
5. Add cider, broth and vinegar to skillet; remove skillet from heat. Bake, covered, 35–40 minutes, until chicken is cooked through. Remove chicken rolls from skillet; let stand, covered, 10 minutes.
6. Transfer vegetable mixture to food processor, blender or food mill; purée until smooth. Return mixture to skillet; cook over high heat, stirring constantly, until mixture is slightly thickened.
7. Carefully remove string from chicken rolls; cut each into 4 equal slices. Serve topped with vegetable mixture.

Each serving provides: ¾ Fat; ¼ Fruit; ½ Vegetable; 3 Proteins; 25 Optional Calories

Per serving: 221 Calories; 25 g Protein; 9 g Fat; 10 g Carbohydrate; 43 mg Calcium; 437 mg Sodium; 61 mg Cholesterol; 1 g Dietary Fiber

WALNUT CHICKEN

Makes 4 servings

Four 3-ounce skinless boneless chicken breasts	1 ounce shelled walnuts, ground or very finely chopped
2 tablespoons oyster sauce*	½ teaspoon dried sage leaves
2 teaspoons prepared mustard	¼ teaspoon black pepper
⅓ cup + 2 teaspoons plain dried bread crumbs	Pinch nutmeg

1. Preheat oven to 425° F. Line large baking sheet with foil; spray with non-stick cooking spray.
2. In large bowl, combine chicken, oyster sauce and mustard, tossing well to coat thoroughly.
3. In gallon-size sealable plastic bag, combine bread crumbs, walnuts, sage, pepper and nutmeg; seal bag and shake to blend. Add 1 chicken breast; seal bag and shake to coat. Place coated chicken breast on prepared baking sheet; repeat, using remaining chicken breasts.
4. Bake 10 minutes; turn chicken breasts over. Bake 5–10 minutes longer, until chicken is golden brown and cooked through.

Each serving provides: ½ Fat; 2¼ Proteins; ½ Bread; 15 Optional Calories

Per serving: 193 Calories; 23 g Protein; 6 g Fat; 10 g Carbohydrate; 46 mg Calcium; 533 mg Sodium; 49 mg Cholesterol; 1 g Dietary Fiber

*Oyster sauce, a thick, dark sauce made of oyster extract and salt, imparts a rich flavor to dishes. It can be purchased in Asian food stores or the Asian food section of some supermarkets.

CHICKEN CHERUBINI

Makes 4 servings

Four 3-ounce skinless boneless
chicken breasts

Four ½-ounce slices cooked
Virginia ham

½ ounce sliced blanched almonds

2 tablespoons minced fresh
flat-leaf parsley

1 tablespoon grated Parmesan
cheese

¼ teaspoon salt

¼ teaspoon black pepper

2 teaspoons corn oil

2 cups thinly sliced mushrooms

½ cup low-sodium chicken broth

½ cup (4 fluid ounces) dry white
wine

2 teaspoons cold unsalted
butter*

1. With sharp knife, slit chicken breasts lengthwise three-quarters of the way
through; spread apart at slit to open. Place each chicken breast, skinned-
side down, between 2 sheets of plastic wrap; with meat mallet, pound chicken
lightly to an even ¼" thickness and set aside.

2. Place 1 ham slice onto each flattened chicken breast. In small bowl,
combine almonds, parsley and Parmesan cheese; spoon an equal amount of
almond mixture onto each ham slice. Roll up chicken breasts to enclose
filling; sprinkle with salt and pepper.

3. In medium skillet, heat oil; add chicken rolls. Cook over medium heat until
golden brown on all sides. Remove chicken rolls from skillet; set aside.

4. To same skillet, add mushrooms; cook, stirring frequently, 7 minutes,
until liquid has evaporated and mushrooms are browned. Add broth and
wine; increase heat to high. Bring liquid to a boil; cook until reduced by
about a third.

5. Return chicken rolls to skillet; reduce heat to low. Cook, covered, 6–8
minutes, until chicken is cooked through, basting frequently. Remove
skillet from heat; transfer chicken rolls to serving platter.

6. Stir butter into pan juices; swirl skillet gently until butter is melted and
mixture thickens slightly. To serve, pour butter mixture over chicken rolls.

Each serving provides: ¾ Fat; 1 Vegetable; 2½ Proteins; 60 Optional
Calories

Per serving: 211 Calories; 25 g Protein; 9 g Fat; 3 g Carbohydrate; 45 mg
Calcium; 395 mg Sodium; 63 mg Cholesterol; 1 g Dietary Fiber

**Stick margarine may be substituted for the butter; increase Fat Selection to 1¼ and reduce
Optional Calories to 45.*

Per serving with stick margarine: 211 Calories; 25 g Protein; 9 g Fat;
3 g Carbohydrate; 45 mg Calcium; 417 mg Sodium; 58 mg Cholesterol;
1 g Dietary Fiber

CHICKEN WITH WHITE GRAPES

Makes 4 servings

2 teaspoons vegetable oil	1 teaspoon white wine vinegar
10 ounces skinless boneless chicken breasts, cut into 8 equal pieces	2 tablespoons minced fresh flat-leaf parsley
20 small seedless white grapes	2 tablespoons nonfat sour cream
½ cup (4 fluid ounces) dry white wine	½ teaspoon salt
	½ teaspoon dried chervil leaves
¼ cup low-sodium chicken broth	¼ teaspoon black pepper

1. In medium skillet, heat oil; add chicken. Cook over medium-high heat 2
   minutes on each side, until golden brown. Remove chicken from skillet;
   set aside.
2. To same skillet, add grapes, wine, broth and vinegar; bring liquid to a boil.
   Reduce heat to medium; add reserved chicken. Cook, basting chicken with
   pan juices, 3–4 minutes, until chicken is cooked through and grapes are
   tender but not mushy. Transfer chicken and grapes to serving platter.
3. Cook broth mixture until reduced to about ½ cup. Stir in parsley, sour cream,
   salt, chervil and pepper; pour over chicken and grapes.

Each serving provides: ½ Fat; ¼ Fruit; 2 Proteins; 30 Optional Calories

Per serving: 141 Calories; 17 g Protein; 3 g Fat; 5 g Carbohydrate; 28 mg
Calcium; 131 mg Sodium; 41 mg Cholesterol; 0 g Dietary Fiber

CHICKEN VERMOUTH WITH GRAPES

Makes 4 servings

Chicken:

Four 4-ounce chicken breasts

1 tablespoon + 1 teaspoon
   aromatic bitters

1 tablespoon grated orange peel

1 teaspoon dried rosemary
   leaves, crushed

½ teaspoon cracked black
   peppercorns

Sauce:

½ cup thinly sliced onion

1 garlic clove, minced

½ cup low-sodium chicken broth

2 tablespoons (1 fluid ounce)
   dry red vermouth

12 large seedless red grapes

1. Preheat broiler. Spray broiler pan with nonstick cooking spray.
2. To prepare chicken, loosen skin of chicken breasts carefully; place in prepared broiler pan, skin-side up.
3. In small bowl, combine aromatic bitters, orange peel, rosemary and peppercorns; spoon under skin and all over sides of chicken breasts. Broil chicken breasts 4" from heat 5 minutes; remove chicken from broiler and set aside.
4. Preheat oven to 350° F. Spray 1-quart baking dish with nonstick cooking spray.
5. To prepare sauce, spray medium skillet with nonstick cooking spray; add onion. Cook over medium heat, stirring frequently, 3–4 minutes, until lightly browned. Add garlic; cook, stirring constantly, 2 minutes longer. Add broth and vermouth; bring liquid to a boil. Cook until mixture is reduced by about half. Stir in grapes; remove from heat.
6. Remove and discard skin from chicken. Place chicken in prepared baking dish; top with sauce. Bake 15–20 minutes, basting often with sauce, until chicken is cooked through and juices run clear when pierced with a fork.
7. To serve, transfer chicken to serving platter; top with sauce.

Each serving provides: ¼ Fruit; ¼ Vegetable; 2 Proteins; 10 Optional Calories

Per serving: 150 Calories; 19 g Protein; 3 g Fat; 7 g Carbohydrate; 24 mg Calcium; 50 mg Sodium; 48 mg Cholesterol; 0 g Dietary Fiber

CHICKEN WITH CRANBERRIES, PRUNES AND APRICOTS

The dark, wine-flavored sauce in this quick stew is brightened with fruit and orange zest; serve it with a sweet-potato purée and sautéed bitter greens, such as mustard or escarole.

Makes 4 servings

1 teaspoon vegetable oil	1 teaspoon cornstarch
Four 6-ounce chicken thighs, skinned	18 dried apricot halves, slivered
1 cup diced onions	½ cup cranberries
½ cup low-sodium chicken broth	6 medium prunes, pitted and chopped
¼ cup (2 fluid ounces) dry red wine	2 teaspoons julienne-cut orange zest*
¼ cup orange juice	1 small bay leaf

1. In medium skillet, heat oil; add chicken. Cook over medium-high heat, turning as needed, until golden brown on all sides. Remove chicken from skillet; set aside.
2. To same skillet, add onions; cook, stirring frequently, 4–5 minutes, until golden brown.
3. In small bowl, with wire whisk, combine broth, wine, orange juice and cornstarch, blending until cornstarch is dissolved; stir into cooked onions. Add reserved chicken, apricots, cranberries, prunes, orange zest and bay leaf; bring liquid to a boil. Reduce heat to low; simmer, basting chicken frequently with pan juices, 20 minutes, until chicken is cooked through and liquid is slightly thickened. Remove and discard bay leaf.

Each serving provides: ¼ Fat; 1½ Fruits; ½ Vegetable; 3 Proteins; 20 Optional Calories

Per serving: 299 Calories; 24 g Protein; 11 g Fat; 25 g Carbohydrate; 38 mg Calcium; 86 mg Sodium; 81 mg Cholesterol; 3 g Dietary Fiber

The zest of the orange is the peel without any of the pith (white membrane). To remove zest from orange, use a zester or vegetable peeler; wrap orange in plastic wrap and refrigerate for use at another time.

STUFFED CHICKEN BREAST

Makes 6 servings

One 1-pound 4-ounce skinless
boneless chicken breast

1 teaspoon olive oil

1 cup finely chopped mushrooms

½ cup cooked spinach,
thoroughly drained and
squeezed dry, chopped

1 garlic clove, minced

½ teaspoon salt

¼ teaspoon crushed red pepper
flakes

1½ ounces smoked mozzarella
cheese, thinly sliced

½ cup low-sodium chicken broth

1½ cups stewed tomatoes

1 tablespoon chopped fresh basil
leaves or ½ teaspoon dried

1. Preheat oven to 375° F. Spray an 8" square baking pan with nonstick cooking spray.
2. Place chicken breast, skinned-side down, between 2 sheets of plastic wrap.
With meat mallet, pound chicken lightly to an even ¾" thickness. Set chicken
aside.
3. In medium skillet, heat oil; add mushrooms. Cook over medium heat, stirring constantly, 5 minutes, until all liquid has evaporated. Add spinach and
garlic; cook, stirring constantly, 2 minutes longer. Stir in salt and crushed
red pepper.
4. Arrange half of the mushroom mixture lengthwise along center of chicken
breast; top evenly with cheese, then the remaining mushroom mixture. Fold
long sides of chicken over stuffing, overlapping slightly. Secure with kitchen
string.
5. Place stuffed chicken breast in prepared baking pan, seam-side down; add
¼ cup of the chicken broth. Bake, covered, 30 minutes, basting once, until
chicken is cooked through and juices run clear when pierced with a fork.
6. While chicken is baking, in blender or food processor, combine tomatoes
and the remaining ¼ cup chicken broth; purée until smooth. Transfer tomato mixture to small saucepan; cook over low heat, stirring occasionally,
5 minutes, until heated. Stir in basil; set aside and keep warm.
7. Let chicken breast stand 10 minutes. Carefully remove string, then slice
into equal pieces. Serve with warm tomato mixture.

Each serving provides: ¾ Vegetable; 3 Proteins; 10 Optional Calories

Per serving: 159 Calories; 25 g Protein; 4 g Fat; 6 g Carbohydrate; 94 mg
Calcium; 448 mg Sodium; 60 mg Cholesterol; 2 g Dietary Fiber

CHICKEN WITH ARTICHOKE HEARTS

Makes 4 servings

3 ounces medium pasta shells	1 cup low-sodium chicken broth
1 ounce pine nuts (pignolias)	¼ cup balsamic vinegar
2 teaspoons olive oil	1 teaspoon dried oregano leaves
Four 3-ounce skinless boneless chicken breasts, pounded thin	1 cup thawed frozen artichoke hearts
1 medium red bell pepper, seeded and cut into strips	¾ ounce feta cheese, crumbled
1 cup thinly sliced mushrooms	2 tablespoons chopped fresh flat-leaf parsley
2 garlic cloves, minced	

1. In large pot of boiling water, cook pasta 9–11 minutes, until tender; drain.
2. While pasta is cooking, in large nonstick skillet, toast pine nuts over medium-high heat 2–3 minutes, until golden brown; transfer to small bowl.
3. In same skillet, heat oil; add chicken. Cook 3–4 minutes on each side, until golden brown and cooked through. Remove chicken from skillet; set aside.
4. To same skillet, add red pepper, mushrooms and garlic; cook, stirring frequently, 4–5 minutes, until tender. Remove vegetables from skillet; set aside.
5. Add broth, vinegar and oregano to same skillet; bring to a boil. Cook 4–5 minutes, until liquid is reduced by about half. Return chicken and vegetables to skillet; add cooked pasta and artichokes. Simmer 2–3 minutes, until flavors are blended.
6. To serve, transfer mixture to serving platter; sprinkle with cheese, reserved pine nuts and parsley.

Each serving provides: 1 Fat; 1½ Vegetables; 2½ Proteins; 1 Bread; 5 Optional Calories

Per serving: 283 Calories; 27 g Protein; 9 g Fat; 24 g Carbohydrate; 63 mg Calcium; 152 mg Sodium; 54 mg Cholesterol; 3 g Dietary Fiber

CHICKEN ROULADES WITH ROASTED VEGETABLES

Roasting the vegetables gives them a deep, rich flavor, which is a lovely counterpoint to the herb-scented chicken.

Makes 4 servings

Chicken:

Four 3-ounce skinless boneless chicken breasts, pounded thin

¼ teaspoon salt

⅛ teaspoon ground white pepper

12 fresh basil leaves

2 tablespoons chopped fresh rosemary

4 garlic cloves

2 teaspoons canola oil

2 medium carrots

2 medium celery stalks

6 ounces minced shallots

1 medium onion, quartered

Pepper Sauce:

¾ cup low-sodium vegetable broth

½ cup chopped onion

1 cup chopped red bell pepper

½ cup chopped tomato

1 tablespoon minced shallots

2 garlic cloves, minced

½ teaspoon dried thyme leaves

½ cup fresh basil leaves

1 tablespoon balsamic vinegar

¼ teaspoon salt

⅛ teaspoon freshly ground black pepper

1. Preheat oven to 375° F.
2. To prepare chicken, sprinkle chicken with salt and white pepper. Place 3 basil leaves on each chicken breast; roll up chicken to enclose leaves.
3. In food processor, combine 1 tablespoon of the rosemary, the garlic and oil; purée until mixture forms a smooth paste. Rub paste evenly over chicken rolls.
4. To food processor, add carrots, celery, shallots and quartered onion; process until coarsely chopped. Transfer vegetable mixture to an 8" square baking pan; arrange chicken rolls on top of vegetables. Roast 20–25 minutes, until chicken is cooked through and vegetables are tender.
5. While chicken is roasting, prepare sauce. In medium saucepan, combine ¼ cup of the broth and the chopped onion; bring liquid to a boil. Reduce heat to low; simmer 5 minutes. Add red pepper, tomato, the remaining ½ cup broth, the shallots, garlic and thyme; bring liquid to a boil. Reduce heat to low; simmer 5–7 minutes, until vegetables are tender.

6. Transfer broth mixture to food processor; add basil, vinegar, salt and black pepper. Purée until mixture is smooth.
7. To serve, divide roasted vegetables evenly among 4 plates. Top each portion with 1 chicken roll and ¼ of the sauce.

Each serving provides: ½ Fat; 3 Vegetables; 2 Proteins; 5 Optional Calories

Per serving: 218 Calories; 23 g Protein; 4 g Fat; 23 g Carbohydrate; 126 mg Calcium; 377 mg Sodium; 49 mg Cholesterol; 4 g Dietary Fiber

CHICKEN JUBILEE

Makes 4 servings

2 teaspoons stick margarine	1 bay leaf
Four 6-ounce chicken thighs, skinned	½ teaspoon dried rosemary leaves
½ cup minced shallots	¼ teaspoon salt
3 tablespoons (1½ fluid ounces) kirsch	¼ teaspoon black pepper
¼ cup (2 fluid ounces) dry red wine	⅛ teaspoon ground cloves
	24 large Bing cherries, pitted
¼ cup low-sodium beef broth	1 teaspoon red wine vinegar

1. In large skillet, heat margarine; add chicken. Cook over medium heat 2 minutes on each side, until golden brown. Add shallots; cook, stirring frequently, until golden brown. Remove skillet from heat.
2. Pour kirsch into skillet; with long match, ignite mixture carefully. Constantly tilting skillet, cook until flames are extinguished. Add wine, broth, bay leaf, rosemary, salt, pepper and cloves; bring to a boil, stirring constantly. Reduce heat to low; simmer, covered, stirring occasionally, 20 minutes, until flavors are blended.
3. Stir in cherries and vinegar; cook 5 minutes, until cherries are softened. Remove and discard bay leaf.

Each serving provides: ½ Fat; ½ Fruit; ¼ Vegetable; 3 Proteins; 45 Optional Calories

Per serving: 281 Calories; 23 g Protein; 12 g Fat; 14 g Carbohydrate; 31 mg Calcium; 236 mg Sodium; 81 mg Cholesterol; 1 g Dietary Fiber

PARTY BAKED CHICKEN

Rich, creamy and delicious, you're certain to enjoy this lighter version of the original dish.

Makes 8 servings

2 teaspoons herbes de Provence*	One 3-pound chicken, skinned and cut into 8 pieces
1 garlic clove, mashed into a purée	¼ cup low-sodium chicken broth
½ teaspoon salt	¼ cup (2 fluid ounces) dry white wine
½ teaspoon black pepper	½ cup light cream cheese

1. Preheat oven to 350° F. Spray a 13 × 9" baking pan with nonstick cooking spray.
2. In small bowl, combine herbes de Provence, garlic, salt and pepper; rub half of mixture over chicken. Place chicken in prepared baking pan; add broth and wine to pan. Bake, tightly covered, 1 hour, until chicken is cooked through and thigh juices run clear when pierced with a fork.
3. While chicken is baking, combine cream cheese and remaining herbes de Provence mixture.
4. Transfer chicken to serving platter; strain pan juices into small saucepan. With wire whisk, blend in cream cheese mixture; continuing to stir with whisk, cook over low heat until warm (do not boil).
5. To serve, pour cream cheese mixture over chicken.

Each serving provides: 2 Proteins; 35 Optional Calories

Per serving: 146 Calories; 18 g Protein; 7 g Fat; 1 g Carbohydrate; 31 mg Calcium; 268 mg Sodium; 58 mg Cholesterol; 0 g Dietary Fiber

*Herbes de Provence, an herb blend typical of southern France, usually combines thyme, bay leaf, rosemary, sage, savory, fennel and/or marjoram. It can be purchased in most gourmet food stores.

CLASSIC CHICKEN PAPRIKASH

This is a variation of the classic dish, having lost nothing but fat. In traditional style, serve it with rice or noodles.

Makes 8 servings

2 teaspoons corn oil	¼ teaspoon black pepper
One 3-pound chicken, skinned and cut into 8 pieces	½ cup low-sodium chicken broth
1 cup sliced onions	¼ cup (2 fluid ounces) dry white wine
2 tablespoons paprika (preferably Hungarian, mild or hot)	2 tablespoons white wine vinegar
2 garlic cloves, minced	1 tablespoon tomato purée
½ teaspoon dried thyme leaves	2 teaspoons all-purpose flour
½ teaspoon salt	½ cup nonfat sour cream

1. In large skillet, heat oil; add chicken. Cook over medium-high heat 2 minutes on each side, until golden brown. Remove chicken from skillet; set aside.
2. To same skillet, add onions; cook, stirring frequently, 4–5 minutes, until onions are lightly browned. Reduce heat to low; add paprika and garlic. Cook, stirring constantly, 3 minutes. Stir in thyme, salt and pepper.
3. In small bowl, with wire whisk, combine broth, wine, vinegar, tomato purée and flour, blending until flour is dissolved; strain and add to onion mixture. Continuing to stir with whisk, bring liquid to a boil over high heat; add reserved chicken. Reduce heat to low; simmer 20 minutes, basting chicken occasionally with pan juices, until chicken is cooked through and thigh juices run clear when pierced with a fork.
4. Transfer chicken to serving platter. With wire whisk, blend sour cream into pan juices; pour over chicken.

Each serving provides: ¼ Fat; ¼ Vegetable; 2 Proteins; 20 Optional Calories

Per serving: 152 Calories; 18 g Protein; 6 g Fat; 5 g Carbohydrate; 40 mg Calcium; 208 mg Sodium; 50 mg Cholesterol; 0 g Dietary Fiber

CHICKEN-FILLED CRÊPES

Makes 4 servings

Crêpes:

½ cup + 1 tablespoon all-purpose flour

½ cup egg substitute

½ cup skim milk

2 teaspoons vegetable oil

⅛ teaspoon salt

Filling:

1 teaspoon vegetable oil

1 cup sliced mushrooms

¼ cup minced onion

½ cup low-sodium chicken broth

¼ cup (2 fluid ounces) dry white wine

½ cup evaporated skimmed milk

1½ teaspoons cornstarch

¼ cup nonfat sour cream

½ teaspoon salt

¼ teaspoon black pepper

⅛ teaspoon dried thyme leaves

10 ounces skinless cooked chicken, shredded or finely diced

Topping:

1 tablespoon + 1 teaspoon grated Parmesan cheese

1. To prepare crêpes, in small bowl, with wire whisk, combine flour, egg substitute, milk, oil and salt, blending until flour is dissolved. Strain into small bowl; refrigerate, covered, 2–8 hours.

2. Spray nonstick crêpe pan with nonstick cooking spray; place over medium-high heat. Stir crêpe batter; pour a scant 3 tablespoons batter into prepared pan, tilting pan until bottom is evenly coated. Cook a few seconds, just until lightly browned on bottom; turn. Cook a few seconds longer, until other side begins to brown. Remove crêpe from skillet; repeat, making 7 more crêpes.

3. To prepare filling, in medium skillet, heat oil; add mushrooms and onion. Cook over medium-high heat, stirring frequently, until all liquid has evaporated and onion is golden brown. Add broth and wine; bring liquid to a boil. Reduce heat to low; simmer, covered, 5 minutes.

4. In small bowl, with wire whisk, combine evaporated skimmed milk and cornstarch, blending until cornstarch is dissolved; stir into broth mixture. Cook, stirring constantly, until mixture is thickened. Remove skillet from heat; stir in sour cream, salt, pepper and thyme. Set aside ⅔ cup mushroom mixture; stir chicken into remaining mixture.

5. Preheat broiler. Spray an 8" square baking pan with nonstick cooking spray.

6. Spoon an equal amount of chicken mixture onto center of each crêpe; roll to enclose filling. Place filled crêpes seam-side down in prepared baking pan; top with reserved mushroom mixture, then sprinkle evenly with Parmesan cheese. Broil 8" from heat 2–3 minutes, until piping hot and top is golden brown.

Each serving (2 filled crêpes) provides: ¼ Milk; ¾ Fat; ¾ Vegetable; 3 Proteins; ¾ Bread; 50 Optional Calories

Per serving: 337 Calories; 31 g Protein; 12 g Fat; 23 g Carbohydrate; 203 mg Calcium; 546 mg Sodium; 66 mg Cholesterol; 1 g Dietary Fiber

CHICKEN PINWHEELS

Makes 4 servings

1 tablespoon + 1 teaspoon reduced-calorie tub margarine

1 cup thinly sliced onions, separated into rings

8 ounces skinless cooked chicken, shredded

1 cup chopped fresh basil leaves

1 cup chopped drained roasted red peppers

1 tablespoon grated Parmesan cheese

8 ounces thawed frozen bread dough

1. Preheat oven to 400° F.
2. In medium nonstick skillet, melt margarine; add onions. Cook, stirring frequently, 2–3 minutes, until softened. Remove from heat; stir in chicken, basil, red peppers and cheese. Set aside.
3. Spray work surface with nonstick cooking spray; with rolling pin, roll bread dough on work surface into a 12 × 9" rectangle.
4. Spoon chicken mixture onto bread dough to within ½" of edges. Starting at a long edge, roll dough jelly-roll fashion to enclose chicken mixture.
5. Place roll seam-side down on nonstick baking sheet; bake 15–20 minutes, until golden brown. Let stand 10 minutes; cut into 12 equal pieces. Serve warm or refrigerate until chilled.

Each serving provides: ½ Fat; 1 Vegetable; 2 Proteins; 2 Breads; 10 Optional Calories

Per serving: 321 Calories; 23 g Protein; 10 g Fat; 36 g Carbohydrate; 150 mg Calcium; 391 mg Sodium; 54 mg Cholesterol; 1 g Dietary Fiber

CHICKEN MARENGO

Legend has it that Napoleon's cook prepared this for his victorious general after the battle of Marengo, using everything available. This recipe substitutes shrimp and heart-shaped croutons for the crayfish, fried eggs and cockscombs that garnished the original dish.

Makes 8 servings

Croutons:

- 1 tablespoon + 1 teaspoon olive oil
- 1 garlic clove, lightly crushed
- 4 ounces firm crustless white bread, cut into eight ½-ounce heart-shaped pieces

Chicken:

- 1 tablespoon + 1 teaspoon olive oil
- One 3-pound chicken, skinned and cut into 8 pieces
- 2 cups quartered mushrooms
- 2 garlic cloves, minced
- 3 tablespoons (1½ fluid ounces) brandy
- ½ cup low-sodium beef broth
- ½ cup (4 fluid ounces) dry white wine
- 2 tablespoons tomato purée
- 2 teaspoons all-purpose flour
- 1 bay leaf
- ½ teaspoon dried thyme leaves
- ½ teaspoon dried marjoram leaves
- ½ teaspoon salt
- ¼ teaspoon black pepper
- 16 medium shrimp, peeled and deveined

1. To prepare croutons, in small skillet, heat oil; add garlic. Cook over medium heat, stirring constantly, until lightly browned. Remove and discard garlic. Add bread to skillet; cook until golden brown on both sides. Remove bread from skillet; set aside.
2. To prepare chicken, in large skillet, heat 2 teaspoons of the oil; add chicken. Cook over medium-high heat until browned on all sides. Remove chicken from skillet; set aside.
3. In same skillet, heat remaining 2 teaspoons oil; add mushrooms. Cook, stirring frequently, until liquid has evaporated and mushrooms are golden brown. Add garlic; cook, stirring constantly, 1 minute longer.
4. Return chicken to skillet. Add brandy; with long match, ignite mixture carefully. Constantly tilting skillet, cook until flames are extinguished.
5. In small bowl, with wire whisk, combine broth, wine, tomato purée and flour, blending until flour is dissolved. Strain and add to mushroom mixture, stirring to combine. Add bay leaf, thyme, marjoram, salt and pepper; cook over medium heat, stirring constantly, until thickened. Reduce heat to low; simmer 20–25 minutes, until chicken is cooked through and thigh juices run clear when pierced with a fork.
6. Add shrimp; cook, stirring frequently, 1 minute, until shrimp turn pink. Remove and discard bay leaf. Serve with reserved heart-shaped croutons.

Each serving provides: 1 Fat; ½ Vegetable; 2½ Proteins; ½ Bread; 30 Optional Calories

Per serving: 251 Calories; 24 g Protein; 10 g Fat; 10 g Carbohydrate; 48 mg Calcium; 321 mg Sodium; 94 mg Cholesterol; 1 g Dietary Fiber

Coq au Vin

Makes 8 servings

1 tablespoon + 1 teaspoon stick margarine

One 3-pound chicken, skinned and cut into 8 pieces

3 cups sliced mushrooms

1 cup frozen baby onions, thawed and drained

2 garlic cloves, minced

3 tablespoons (1½ fluid ounces) brandy

½ cup (4 fluid ounces) dry red wine

2 tablespoons minced fresh flat-leaf parsley

½ teaspoon dried thyme leaves

½ teaspoon dried chervil leaves

½ teaspoon salt

¼ teaspoon black pepper

½ teaspoon cornstarch, dissolved in 1 tablespoon cold water

1. In large skillet, heat 2 teaspoons of the margarine; add chicken. Cook over medium-high heat 2 minutes on each side, until golden brown. Remove chicken from skillet; set aside.

2. In same skillet, heat remaining 2 teaspoons margarine; add mushrooms and onions. Cook, stirring frequently, 4–5 minutes, until onions are golden brown. Add garlic; cook, stirring constantly, 2 minutes longer.

3. Pour brandy into skillet; with long match, ignite mixture carefully. Constantly tilting skillet, cook until flames are extinguished.

4. Return chicken to skillet; add wine, parsley, thyme, chervil, salt and pepper. Bring liquid to a boil; reduce heat to low. Simmer, covered, 20 minutes, stirring occasionally, until chicken is cooked through and thigh juices run clear when pierced with a fork.

5. Stir in dissolved cornstarch; cook over high heat 2 minutes, until sauce is slightly reduced and thickened.

Each serving provides: ½ Fat; 1 Vegetable; 2 Proteins; 30 Optional Calories

Per serving: 166 Calories; 18 g Protein; 6 g Fat; 4 g Carbohydrate; 25 mg Calcium; 212 mg Sodium; 50 mg Cholesterol; 0 g Dietary Fiber

CHICKEN QUENELLES

Makes 4 servings

Quenelles:

10 ounces skinless boneless
chicken breasts, diced

3 egg whites

½ teaspoon salt

¼ teaspoon black pepper

Pinch nutmeg

½ cup evaporated skimmed milk

Sauce:

2 teaspoons unsalted butter*

½ cup sliced mushrooms

2 tablespoons minced onion

½ cup low-sodium chicken broth

½ cup evaporated skimmed milk

1 tablespoon all-purpose flour

Pinch ground red pepper

1. To prepare quenelles, in food processor, combine chicken, egg whites, salt, black pepper and nutmeg; process 30 seconds. Continuing to process, slowly add milk, processing 1 minute longer, until very smooth.
2. In large, deep skillet, bring 2" salted water to a boil; reduce heat to low. Using 2 soup spoons, form chicken mixture into 12 ovals; slide ovals into simmering water. Cook 5–7 minutes, just until ovals are firm to the touch. Remove ovals from water; drain on paper towels. Set aside; keep warm.
3. To prepare sauce, in small saucepan, heat butter; add mushrooms and onion. Cook over medium heat, stirring frequently, 4 minutes, until vegetables are soft.
4. In small bowl, with wire whisk, combine broth, milk, flour and ground red pepper, blending until flour is dissolved; strain and add to mushroom mixture. Stirring constantly, bring mixture to a boil; reduce heat. Simmer, stirring often, 15 minutes, until thickened. Serve sauce over quenelles.

Each serving (3 quenelles with ⅓ cup sauce) provides: ½ Milk; ¼ Vegetable; 2¼ Proteins; 30 Optional Calories

Per serving: 173 Calories; 25 g Protein; 3 g Fat; 10 g Carbohydrate; 200 mg Calcium; 580 mg Sodium; 49 mg Cholesterol; 0 g Dietary Fiber

*Stick margarine may be substituted for the butter; add ½ Fat Selection and reduce Optional Calories to 10.

Per serving with stick margarine: 173 Calories; 25 g Protein; 3 g Fat; 10 g Carbohydrate; 200 mg Calcium; 602 mg Sodium; 44 mg Cholesterol; 0 g Dietary Fiber

TERRINE OF CHICKEN AND VEAL

For the best flavor, make this easy terrine a day or two before you serve it. A wonderful first course or part of an elegant buffet, it should be served with cornichons (tiny French pickles), Dijon-style mustard and fresh French bread.

Makes 16 servings

4 ounces skinless boneless chicken breasts, diced

2 ounces cooked Virginia ham, finely diced

¼ cup (2 fluid ounces) dry sherry

8 ounces skinless boneless chicken thighs, cubed

4 ounces boneless veal or skinless boneless chicken breasts, cubed

1 egg, beaten

1 tablespoon + 1 teaspoon unsalted butter*

2 teaspoons vegetable oil

2 ounces chicken liver

¾ teaspoon salt

½ teaspoon ground ginger

¼ teaspoon black pepper, or to taste

⅛ teaspoon ground nutmeg

½ cup minced fresh flat-leaf parsley to garnish

1. In small bowl, combine diced chicken breasts, ham and 2 tablespoons of the sherry; let stand, covered, 2 hours.
2. Adjust oven rack to divide oven in half; preheat oven to 350° F. Spray an 8 × 4" loaf pan with nonstick cooking spray.
3. In food processor, combine chicken thighs, veal and egg; process until coarsely ground. Set aside.

4. In small saucepan, heat butter and oil; when foam subsides, add liver. Cook, stirring frequently, 3 minutes, until no longer pink. Remove skillet from heat; mash liver with a fork.

5. In medium bowl, with wooden spoon, combine ground chicken mixture, mashed liver along with any pan juices, the remaining sherry, the salt, ginger, pepper and nutmeg; beating well, fold in reserved diced chicken mixture. Spoon mixture into prepared loaf pan, pressing down firmly. Cover pan tightly with foil.

6. Place loaf pan in large roasting pan; set on center of oven rack. Pour boiling water carefully into roasting pan to a depth of about 1½". Bake 50 minutes, until mixture is firm and cooked through.

7. Remove loaf pan from water bath; loosen foil cover. Cool slightly, then refrigerate 1 hour. Cover tightly; refrigerate 24–48 hours.

8. To serve, run a spatula around edges of loaf to loosen; unmold onto serving platter. Remove and discard any congealed liquid; sprinkle top and sides of loaf with parsley.

Each serving provides: 1 Protein; 15 Optional Calories

Per serving: 67 Calories; 8 g Protein; 2 g Fat; 1 g Carbohydrate; 9 mg Calcium; 175 mg Sodium; 55 mg Cholesterol; 0 g Dietary Fiber

*Stick margarine may be substituted for the butter; add ¼ Fat Selection and reduce Optional Calories to 10.

Per serving with stick margarine: 67 Calories; 8 g Protein; 2 g Fat; 1 g Carbohydrate; 9 mg Calcium; 184 mg Sodium; 52 mg Cholesterol; 0 g Dietary Fiber

BROCCOLI QUICHE

Makes 4 servings

6 ounces skinless cooked chicken, diced

2 cups thawed frozen chopped broccoli (one 10-ounce box), squeezed of excess liquid

1 cup part-skim ricotta cheese

½ cup egg substitute

⅓ cup + 2 teaspoons plain nonfat yogurt

3 tablespoons all-purpose flour

1 tablespoon + 1 teaspoon stick margarine, melted

2 tablespoons grated Parmesan cheese

½ teaspoon double-acting baking powder

¼ teaspoon salt

1. Preheat oven to 350° F. Spray a 9" pie plate with nonstick cooking spray.
2. In pie plate, combine ½ the chicken and ½ the broccoli. In food processor or blender, combine ricotta cheese, egg substitute, yogurt, flour, margarine, Parmesan cheese, baking powder and salt; purée until smooth. Spoon cheese mixture over chicken and broccoli in pie plate; sprinkle with remaining chicken and broccoli.
3. Bake 30–45 minutes, until toothpick inserted in center comes out clean.

Each serving provides: 1 Fat; 1 Vegetable; 3 Proteins; ¼ Bread; 25 Optional Calories

Per serving: 277 Calories; 27 g Protein; 13 g Fat; 13 g Carbohydrate; 337 mg Calcium; 473 mg Sodium; 59 mg Cholesterol; 1 g Dietary Fiber

10

Ethnic and
Regional Favorites

Chicken Tacos
Chicken-Chili Tacos
Tamale Pie
Chicken Molé
Chicken Enchiladas Molé
Chicken Andree
Chicken with Sausage and Peppers
Risotto with Chicken and Tarragon
Provolone Cutlets with Tomato-Mushroom Sauce
Pasta Paella
Chicken à la Grecque
Chicken Cutlet Paprikash
Chicken Pojarski
Moroccan Chicken
Chicken with Bulgur
Cornish Hens Adrianna
Chicken Argentine
Creole Chicken
Chicken Andouille

Chicken Tacos

Makes 4 servings

2 teaspoons vegetable oil

1 cup chopped green bell pepper

1 cup chopped scallions

2 garlic cloves, minced

10 ounces ground chicken

½ teaspoon ground cumin

¼ teaspoon ground coriander

1½ cups salsa

2 tablespoons chopped fresh cilantro leaves

1 teaspoon mild or hot chili powder

Eight ½-ounce taco shells

2½ cups shredded iceberg lettuce

½ cup nonfat sour cream

1½ ounces cheddar cheese, shredded

10 small pitted black olives, sliced

1. Preheat oven to 350° F.
2. In large nonstick skillet, heat oil; add green pepper, scallions and garlic. Cook, stirring frequently, 2–3 minutes, until vegetables are softened. Add chicken; cook, stirring to break up meat, 4–5 minutes, until no longer pink.
3. Stir cumin and coriander into chicken mixture; cook, stirring frequently, 1 minute. Add salsa, cilantro and chili powder; cook, partially covered, 10 minutes. Uncover; cook 5–7 minutes longer, until mixture is thick but not dry.
4. While chicken mixture is cooking, arrange taco shells on baking sheet; bake 6–8 minutes, until heated and crisp.
5. To serve, divide chicken mixture evenly among taco shells. Top evenly with lettuce, sour cream, cheese and olives.

Each serving provides: ¾ Fat; 2¼ Vegetables; 2½ Proteins; 1 Bread; 20 Optional Calories

Per serving: 391 Calories; 20 g Protein; 19 g Fat; 34 g Carbohydrate; 237 mg Calcium; 970 mg Sodium; 70 mg Cholesterol; 4 g Dietary Fiber

CHICKEN-CHILI TACOS

Makes 4 servings

1 medium onion, chopped

2 garlic cloves, minced

10 ounces ground chicken

1 medium red bell pepper, seeded and chopped

2 cups canned crushed tomatoes

½ teaspoon mild or hot chili powder

½ teaspoon ground cumin

¼ teaspoon coarsely ground black pepper

8 ounces drained cooked red kidney beans

Eight ½-ounce taco shells

¼ cup nonfat sour cream

¼ medium avocado, peeled and diced

Fresh cilantro leaves to garnish

1. Preheat oven to 350° F.
2. Spray medium saucepan with nonstick cooking spray; place over medium heat. Add onion and garlic; cook, stirring frequently, 2–3 minutes, until softened.
3. Add chicken and red pepper to onion mixture; cook, stirring to break up meat, 4–5 minutes, until no longer pink and red pepper is soft. Add tomatoes, ½ cup water, chili powder, cumin and black pepper; bring mixture to a boil. Reduce heat to low; simmer 15 minutes.
4. Add beans to chicken mixture; cook, stirring frequently, until heated through.
5. Arrange taco shells on baking sheet; bake 6–8 minutes, until heated and crisp.
6. To serve, divide chicken mixture evenly among taco shells. Top evenly with sour cream and avocado; garnish with cilantro.

Each serving provides: ½ Fat; 1¾ Vegetables; 3 Proteins; 1 Bread; 10 Optional Calories

Per serving: 398 Calories; 22 g Protein; 15 g Fat; 44 g Carbohydrate; 139 mg Calcium; 480 mg Sodium; 59 mg Cholesterol; 6 g Dietary Fiber

TAMALE PIE

Makes 6 servings

Filling:

1 teaspoon corn oil

10 ounces skinless boneless chicken breasts, finely diced

1½ cups diced onions

1 cup diced green bell pepper

1 cup fresh or frozen whole-kernel corn

1 cup tomato sauce

½ cup low-sodium chicken broth

2 teaspoons mild or hot chili powder

1 teaspoon ground cumin

1 teaspoon dried oregano leaves

Topping:

1 cup minus 1 tablespoon uncooked cornmeal

¾ cup fresh or frozen whole-kernel corn

3 tablespoons all-purpose flour

1½ ounces extra-sharp cheddar cheese, shredded

¾ ounce grated Parmesan cheese

1¼ teaspoons double-acting baking powder

¼ teaspoon salt

1 cup skim buttermilk

1 egg, beaten

2 teaspoons seeded and minced jalapeño pepper, or to taste

1. Adjust oven racks to divide oven into thirds; preheat oven to 425° F. Spray an 8" square baking pan with nonstick cooking spray.

2. To prepare filling, in medium skillet, heat oil; add chicken. Cook over medium heat, stirring frequently, 3–4 minutes, until cooked through and lightly browned. Remove chicken from skillet; set aside.

3. To same skillet, add onions and green pepper; cook, stirring frequently, 4–5 minutes, until onions are golden brown. Return chicken to skillet; stir in corn, tomato sauce, broth, chili powder, cumin and oregano. Bring liquid to a boil; reduce heat to low. Simmer 10 minutes, until mixture thickens slightly and flavors are blended.

4. To prepare topping, in medium bowl, combine cornmeal, corn, flour, cheddar and Parmesan cheeses, baking powder and salt. In small bowl, combine buttermilk, egg and jalapeño pepper. Add egg mixture to cornmeal mixture; stir just until blended.

5. Pour chicken mixture into prepared baking pan; top evenly with spoonsful of topping. Bake in upper third of oven 20–25 minutes, until topping is golden brown and mixture is bubbling.

Each serving provides: 1½ Vegetables; 2 Proteins; 2 Breads; 25 Optional Calories

Per serving: 305 Calories; 22 g Protein; 7 g Fat; 39 g Carbohydrate; 241 mg Calcium; 654 mg Sodium; 75 mg Cholesterol; 4 g Dietary Fiber

CHICKEN MOLÉ

Makes 8 servings

1 cup low-sodium chicken broth	2 teaspoons sesame seeds
One 3-pound chicken, skinned and cut into 8 pieces	1 teaspoon aniseed
	2 garlic cloves, minced
½ cup diced onion	1 cup stewed tomatoes
2 tablespoons raisins	1 tablespoon unsweetened cocoa powder
2 medium jalapeño peppers, or to taste	¼ teaspoon cinnamon
½ ounce shelled almonds	

1. Preheat oven to 350° F.
2. In medium ovenproof skillet, bring broth to a simmer over low heat; add chicken. Cook, covered, 10 minutes. Remove skillet from heat; set aside.
3. In food processor or blender, combine onion and raisins. On long metal fork, toast jalapeño peppers over an open flame, turning frequently, until charred on all sides. Transfer peppers to sealable plastic bag; seal. Let steam 15 minutes. Wearing rubber gloves, peel and seed peppers; add to onion mixture in food processor.
4. In small skillet, toast almonds, sesame seeds and aniseed over low heat, stirring constantly, until fragrant (do not burn); add to onion mixture.
5. Add garlic to onion mixture; process 30 seconds. Add ½ cup of the tomatoes; process just to combine. Add remaining ½ cup tomatoes; purée.
6. With food processor on, pour reserved broth slowly from chicken into onion mixture, processing until mixture is smooth. Transfer mixture to small skillet; bring to a boil. Reduce heat to low; simmer, stirring frequently, 10 minutes. In small cup, combine cocoa and cinnamon; stir into onion mixture.
7. Pour onion mixture over chicken in skillet; bake, covered, 30 minutes, until chicken is cooked through and thigh juices run clear when pierced.

Each serving provides: ¾ Vegetable; 2 Proteins; 25 Optional Calories

Per serving: 150 Calories; 18 g Protein; 6 g Fat; 7 g Carbohydrate; 40 mg Calcium; 138 mg Sodium; 51 mg Cholesterol; 1 g Dietary Fiber

CHICKEN ENCHILADAS MOLÉ

Makes 4 servings

2 large plum tomatoes

1 medium green bell pepper

1 medium jalapeño pepper

½ medium barely ripe banana (yellow with some green), thickly sliced

½ ounce shelled walnuts

1 large garlic clove

¾ cup low-sodium chicken broth

¼ teaspoon cinnamon

⅛ teaspoon ground cloves

⅛ teaspoon dried oregano leaves

⅛ teaspoon salt

Eight 6" corn tortillas

8 ounces skinless cooked chicken, finely shredded

3 ounces Muenster or Monterey Jack cheese, shredded

Thin red onion slices to garnish

1. Preheat broiler. Line large baking sheet with foil; spray with nonstick cooking spray.
2. Arrange tomatoes, green pepper, jalapeño pepper, banana, walnuts and garlic on prepared baking sheet, keeping them separate.
3. Broil 4" from heat, checking frequently and turning as needed, 1–2 minutes for walnuts and garlic, 1 minute on each side for banana and 3 minutes on each side for tomatoes and peppers, until evenly toasted (be careful not to scorch). When cool enough to handle, wearing rubber gloves, core and seed peppers; transfer to blender or food processor, along with other toasted ingredients.
4. Add ¼ cup of the broth, the cinnamon, cloves, oregano and salt to blender; purée until smooth, gradually adding remaining broth.
5. Preheat oven to 425° F. Spray a 2-quart shallow baking dish with nonstick cooking spray.
6. Spread each tortilla with 2 teaspoons of the vegetable mixture; top each with an equal amount of chicken. Roll up tortillas to enclose filling.
7. Arrange tortillas, seam-side down, in a single layer in prepared baking dish; top with remaining vegetable mixture. Bake 15 minutes. Sprinkle with cheese; bake 5 minutes longer, just until cheese is melted. Serve garnished with red onion slices.

Each serving (2 enchiladas) provides: ¼ Fat; ¼ Fruit; 1¼ Vegetables; 3 Proteins; 2 Breads; 10 Optional Calories

Per serving: 357 Calories; 26 g Protein; 15 g Fat; 31 g Carbohydrate; 262 mg Calcium; 346 mg Sodium; 71 mg Cholesterol; 4 g Dietary Fiber

CHICKEN ANDREE

Depending upon how many jalapeños you use, this dish can be just a little spicy, or very incendiary indeed; our version is moderately hot.

Makes 4 servings

2 medium jalapeño peppers, or to taste

3 tablespoons unsalted, shelled, raw pumpkin seeds*

1 medium white onion, quartered

¼ cup minced fresh cilantro leaves

1 garlic clove, minced

½ cup low-sodium chicken broth

2 teaspoons stick margarine

10 ounces skinless boneless chicken breasts, cut into 8 equal pieces

¼ cup nonfat sour cream

1. Preheat broiler. Line large baking sheet with foil.
2. Place jalapeño peppers on prepared baking sheet; broil 4" from heat, turning frequently, until blistered on all sides. Transfer peppers to sealable plastic bag; let steam 15 minutes. Wearing rubber gloves, peel, seed and rinse steamed peppers; transfer to blender or food processor.
3. In medium skillet, toast pumpkin seeds over low heat, stirring constantly, until they begin to pop (do not brown). Add to blender or food processor with jalapeño peppers.
4. To mixture in blender, add onion, 2 tablespoons of the cilantro and the garlic; purée, gradually adding broth, until smooth.
5. In medium skillet, heat margarine; add chicken. Cook over medium heat 2 minutes on each side, until golden brown. Remove chicken from skillet; set aside.
6. To same skillet, add jalapeño pepper mixture. Bring just to a boil; reduce heat to low. Simmer, stirring frequently, 10 minutes (mixture will be thick). Stir in sour cream; add reserved chicken and remaining cilantro. Cook, covered, basting frequently, 3–5 minutes, until chicken is cooked through.

Each serving provides: ½ Fat; ¾ Vegetable; 2 Proteins; 45 Optional Calories

Per serving: 150 Calories; 20 g Protein; 5 g Fat; 6 g Carbohydrate; 38 mg Calcium; 83 mg Sodium; 48 mg Cholesterol; 0 g Dietary Fiber

Unsalted, raw, shelled pumpkin seeds can be purchased in health food stores.

CHICKEN WITH SAUSAGE AND PEPPERS

Makes 4 servings

2 teaspoons olive oil

8 ounces skinless boneless chicken breasts, cut into bite-size pieces

3 ounces lean sweet or hot Italian turkey sausage (10% or less fat)

1 cup sliced onions

1 cup sliced green bell pepper

1 cup sliced red bell pepper

½ cup tomato purée

½ cup low-sodium chicken broth

¼ cup (2 fluid ounces) dry red wine

10 small pitted black olives, coarsely chopped

½ teaspoon dried oregano leaves

¼ teaspoon crushed red pepper flakes

2 tablespoons minced fresh flat-leaf parsley

1. In large skillet, heat oil; add chicken and sausage. Cook over medium-high heat until golden brown on all sides. Remove chicken and sausage from skillet; slice sausage ¼" thick. Set aside.

2. To same skillet, add onions and green and red peppers; cook, stirring frequently, 4–5 minutes, until onions are golden brown. Add tomato purée broth, wine, olives and reserved sausage; bring liquid to a boil. Reduce hea to medium-low; simmer 10 minutes.

3. Add oregano, crushed red pepper and reserved chicken to sausage mixture cook, stirring frequently, 5 minutes, until chicken and sausage are cooked through. Serve sprinkled with parsley.

Each serving provides: ¼ Fat; 2 Vegetables; 2 Proteins; 15 Optional Calories

Per serving: 183 Calories; 18 g Protein; 6 g Fat; 11 g Carbohydrate; 36 mg Calcium; 382 mg Sodium; 48 mg Cholesterol; 2 g Dietary Fiber

RISOTTO WITH CHICKEN AND TARRAGON

Makes 4 servings

1 cup chopped onion	1 tablespoon chopped fresh tarragon leaves or ½ teaspoon dried
2 teaspoons olive oil	
4 ounces arborio (short-grain) rice	
1 cup low-sodium chicken broth	¼ teaspoon salt
10 ounces ground chicken	⅛ teaspoon freshly ground black pepper
1 cup diced celery	

1. In a 2-quart microwave-safe casserole, combine onion and oil; microwave on High 2 minutes, until onion is tender. Add rice; microwave on High 1 minute.
2. Stir broth and ¼ cup water into rice mixture; microwave on High 5–6 minutes, until liquid comes to a boil. Stir in chicken, celery, tarragon, salt and pepper; microwave on High, stirring once to break up meat, 7 minutes, until no longer pink. Remove casserole from oven; let stand, covered, 10 minutes, until liquid is absorbed.

Each serving provides: ½ Fat; 1 Vegetable; 2 Proteins; 1 Bread; 5 Optional Calories

Per serving: 259 Calories; 16 g Protein; 9 g Fat; 27 g Carbohydrate; 43 mg Calcium; 234 mg Sodium; 59 mg Cholesterol; 1 g Dietary Fiber

Provolone Cutlets with Tomato-Mushroom Sauce

Makes 4 servings

2 teaspoons olive oil

½ cup chopped scallions

2 garlic cloves, minced

½ cup sliced mushrooms

½ cup chopped tomato

½ cup chopped green bell pepper

¼ cup chopped fresh basil leaves

Four 3-ounce skinless boneless chicken breasts, pounded thin

¼ teaspoon salt

⅛ teaspoon freshly ground black pepper

1½ ounces provolone cheese, shredded

1. Preheat broiler. Spray rack in broiler pan with nonstick cooking spray.
2. In medium nonstick skillet, heat oil; add scallions and garlic. Cook, stirring frequently, 2–3 minutes, until tender. Stir in mushrooms, tomato, green pepper and basil; cook, stirring frequently, 4–5 minutes, until liquid evaporates. Remove skillet from heat; set aside, covered.
3. Sprinkle chicken with salt and black pepper; place on prepared rack. Broil 4" from heat 3–4 minutes on each side, until lightly browned. Sprinkle chicken evenly with cheese; broil 2 minutes longer, until cheese is melted and chicken is cooked through. Serve topped with vegetable mixture.

Each serving provides: ½ Fat; 1 Vegetable; 2½ Proteins

Per serving: 172 Calories; 23 g Protein; 7 g Fat; 5 g Carbohydrate; 129 mg Calcium; 289 mg Sodium; 57 mg Cholesterol; 1 g Dietary Fiber

Pasta Paella

repared in the microwave, this usually laborious Spanish dish becomes a
0-minute dinner.

Makes 4 servings

5 ounces skinless boneless chicken breast, cut into ½" pieces	3 ounces uncooked tubettini pasta
5 ounces lean hot Italian turkey sausage (10% or less fat), cut into ½" pieces	2 garlic cloves, minced
	½ teaspoon dried thyme leaves
¾ cup low-sodium chicken broth	¼ teaspoon salt
1 cup chopped red bell pepper	⅛ teaspoon powdered saffron
1 cup chopped scallions	2 drops hot pepper sauce, or to taste
	2 cups broccoli florets

1. In a 2-quart microwave-safe casserole, combine chicken, sausage and broth; microwave, covered, on High 4 minutes, stirring once.
2. Stir red pepper, scallions, pasta, garlic, thyme, salt, saffron and hot pepper sauce into chicken mixture; microwave, covered, on Medium 10 minutes, stirring once.
3. Stir broccoli into chicken mixture; microwave, covered, on Medium 6–8 minutes, until broccoli and pasta are tender. Let stand, covered, 10 minutes.

Each serving provides: 2 Vegetables; 2 Proteins; 1 Bread; 5 Optional Calories

Per serving: 219 Calories; 20 g Protein; 5 g Fat; 24 g Carbohydrate; 63 mg Calcium; 383 mg Sodium; 50 mg Cholesterol; 4 g Dietary Fiber

Chicken à la Grecque

The flavors of cinnamon, tomato and feta cheese will bring to mind visions of Athens. Serve this classical dish with warm pitas, a cool salad and a glass of retsina the white wine of Greece.

Makes 8 servings

2 teaspoons olive oil	¼ teaspoon cinnamon
2 cups frozen baby onions, thawed and drained	One 3-pound chicken, skinned and cut into 8 pieces
2 cups tomato sauce	3 ounces feta cheese, crumbled
20 small black olives, pitted and coarsely chopped	

1. Preheat oven to 350° F. Spray an 8" square baking pan with nonstick cooking spray.
2. In large skillet, heat oil; add onions. Cook over medium-high heat, stirring frequently, 3–4 minutes, until lightly browned. Stir in tomato sauce, olive and cinnamon.
3. Place chicken in prepared baking pan; top with tomato sauce mixture. Bake covered, 1 hour, until chicken is cooked through; uncover. Top with cheese bake 5 minutes longer.

Each serving provides: ½ Fat; 1½ Vegetables; 2½ Proteins

Per serving: 188 Calories; 19 g Protein; 9 g Fat; 9 g Carbohydrate; 92 mg Calcium; 602 mg Sodium; 60 mg Cholesterol; 1 g Dietary Fiber

HICKEN CUTLET PAPRIKASH

veet paprika from Hungary will add an authentic note to this dish.

akes 4 servings

Four 3-ounce skinless boneless
  chicken breasts
¼ teaspoon salt
¼ teaspoon freshly ground black
  pepper
2 teaspoons olive oil
1 cup chopped scallions
1 cup chopped red bell pepper

2 garlic cloves, minced
1 tablespoon paprika
½ teaspoon dried thyme leaves
1 cup low-sodium chicken broth
½ cup light sour cream
2 cups hot cooked long-grain
  rice

1. Sprinkle chicken with salt and black pepper; set aside.
2. In large nonstick skillet, heat oil; add chicken. Cook 3–4 minutes on each
   side, until golden brown and cooked through. Remove chicken from skillet; keep warm.
3. To same skillet, add scallions, red pepper and garlic; cook, stirring frequently,
   4–5 minutes, until tender. Stir in paprika and thyme; cook, stirring constantly, 1 minute longer. Stir in broth; bring liquid to a boil. Reduce heat
   to low; simmer 5 minutes, until liquid is reduced by about half. Stir in sour
   cream; simmer 1–2 minutes, until heated through.
4. To serve, spoon rice onto serving platter; top with chicken, then broth
   mixture.

ach serving provides: ½ Fat; 1 Vegetable; 2 Proteins; 1 Bread; 45 Optional
  Calories

er serving: 326 Calories; 26 g Protein; 8 g Fat; 36 g Carbohydrate; 51 mg
  Calcium; 211 mg Sodium; 59 mg Cholesterol; 1 g Dietary Fiber

CHICKEN POJARSKI

Makes 4 servings

1 teaspoon vegetable oil

Four 6-ounce chicken thighs, skinned

½ cup minced onion

1 garlic clove, minced

8 large pitted prunes, halved

½ cup low-sodium chicken broth

¼ cup (2 fluid ounces) tawny port wine

1 teaspoon red wine vinegar

½ teaspoon salt

1 small Granny Smith apple, cored and sliced

¼ teaspoon black pepper

1. In medium skillet, heat oil; add chicken. Cook over medium-high he 2 minutes on each side, until golden brown. Add onion; cook, stirring co stantly, until lightly browned. Add garlic; cook, stirring constantly, 1 minu longer.

2. Add prunes, broth, port, vinegar and salt; bring to a boil. Reduce heat low; simmer 10–15 minutes, basting chicken frequently with pan juice until chicken is cooked through. Transfer chicken to serving platter; kee warm.

3. Add apple and pepper to pan juices; cook, stirring constantly, 5 minute until apple is tender and liquid is slightly thickened. Pour apple mixtu over chicken.

Each serving provides: ¼ Fat; 1¼ Fruits; ¼ Vegetable; 3 Proteins; 25 Optional Calories

Per serving: 290 Calories; 23 g Protein; 11 g Fat; 21 g Carbohydrate; 32 m Calcium; 358 mg Sodium; 81 mg Cholesterol; 2 g Dietary Fiber

MOROCCAN CHICKEN

Cinnamon and fruit give these chicken breasts an exotic flavor.

Makes 4 servings

1 tablespoon + 1 teaspoon olive oil

Four 3-ounce skinless boneless chicken breasts, pounded thin

1 cup chopped onion

1 cup shredded zucchini

2 garlic cloves, minced

2 tablespoons chopped fresh cilantro leaves

½ teaspoon cinnamon

1 cup low-sodium chicken broth

8 ounces drained cooked chick-peas

¼ cup golden raisins

6 medium prunes, pitted and coarsely chopped

2 tablespoons orange juice

1. In large nonstick skillet, heat oil; add chicken. Cook 2 minutes on each side, until golden brown. Remove chicken from skillet; set aside.
2. To same skillet, add onion, zucchini and garlic; cook, stirring frequently, 3–4 minutes, until tender. Stir in cilantro and cinnamon; cook, stirring frequently, 1 minute. Add broth; bring liquid to a boil.
3. Return chicken to skillet; stir in chick-peas, raisins and prunes. Reduce heat to low; simmer, covered, 10 minutes. Stir in orange juice; simmer 5 minutes longer, until chicken is cooked through and mixture is thickened.

Each serving provides: 1 Fat; 1 Fruit; 1 Vegetable; 2 Proteins; 1 Bread; 10 Optional Calories

Per serving: 326 Calories; 27 g Protein; 8 g Fat; 39 g Carbohydrate; 70 mg Calcium; 77 mg Sodium; 49 mg Cholesterol; 4 g Dietary Fiber

Chicken with Bulgur

Makes 4 servings

2 teaspoons vegetable oil

1 cup minced onions

4 ounces uncooked bulgur (cracked wheat)

1 ounce slivered almonds

2 cups low-sodium chicken broth

6 dried apricot halves, slivered

2 tablespoons raisins

½ teaspoon salt

½ teaspoon dried marjoram leaves

¼ teaspoon saffron threads or pinch powdered saffron

⅛ teaspoon cinnamon

7 ounces skinless cooked chicken breasts, julienne-cut

1. In medium nonstick skillet, heat oil; add onions. Cook, stirring frequently, 4–5 minutes, until onions are golden brown. Add bulgur and almonds; cook, stirring constantly, 3 minutes, until almonds are lightly toasted.
2. Add broth, apricots, raisins, salt, marjoram, saffron and cinnamon to bulgur mixture; bring liquid to a simmer. Reduce heat to low; cook, covered, 15 minutes.
3. Add chicken to bulgur mixture; let stand, covered, 15 minutes longer. Fluff mixture with a fork before serving.

Each serving provides: 1 Fat; ½ Fruit; ½ Vegetable; 2 Proteins; 1 Bread; 10 Optional Calories

Per serving: 298 Calories; 22 g Protein; 9 g Fat; 43 g Carbohydrate; 53 mg Calcium; 345 mg Sodium; 42 mg Cholesterol; 7 g Dietary Fiber

CORNISH HENS ADRIANNA

Makes 4 servings

¼ cup minced fresh garlic
2 teaspoons olive oil
2 teaspoons ground cumin
1½ teaspoons salt
1 teaspoon ground bay leaf*
½ teaspoon ground cardamom
¼ teaspoon ground cloves

Two 1-pound Cornish game hens, skinned and halved†
1¼ cups low-sodium chicken broth
4 ounces uncooked brown rice
1 ounce slivered almonds
2 tablespoons raisins

1. Preheat oven to 375° F. Spray a 13 × 9" baking pan with nonstick cooking spray.
2. In small skillet, combine garlic, oil, cumin, salt, bay leaf, cardamom and cloves. Cook over low heat, stirring constantly, 5 minutes, being careful not to allow garlic to brown. Set aside 2 teaspoons of garlic mixture; rub remaining mixture over hens.
3. In prepared baking pan, combine broth, rice, almonds, raisins and reserved garlic mixture. Set hen halves, cut-side down, over rice mixture. Bake, tightly covered, 45–55 minutes, until rice is tender, hens are cooked through and thigh juices run clear when pierced with a fork.

Each serving provides: 1 Fat; ¼ Fruit; 3¼ Proteins; 1 Bread; 5 Optional Calories

Per serving: 373 Calories; 30 g Protein; 14 g Fat; 31 g Carbohydrate; 76 mg Calcium; 920 mg Sodium; 76 mg Cholesterol; 2 g Dietary Fiber

If ground bay leaf is unavailable, you may substitute 2 medium bay leaves, finely ground in a spice blender.

†*A 1-pound Cornish game hen will yield about 6 ounces cooked poultry.*

CHICKEN ARGENTINE

Makes 4 servings

1 tablespoon + 1 teaspoon olive oil

10 ounces skinless boneless chicken breasts, cut into 8 equal pieces

½ teaspoon dried thyme leaves

½ teaspoon dried marjoram leaves

½ teaspoon dried chervil leaves

½ teaspoon crushed green peppercorns

¼ teaspoon dried rosemary leaves, crushed

¼ teaspoon dried sage leaves

⅛ teaspoon ground cloves

⅛ teaspoon ground red pepper (optional)

½ cup orange juice

¼ cup low-sodium chicken broth

3 tablespoons gin

1 small orange, sliced, to garnish

1. In medium skillet, heat oil; add chicken. Cook 2 minutes on each side, until golden brown. Add thyme, marjoram, chervil, green peppercorns, rosemary, sage, cloves and ground red pepper, if using; cook, stirring constantly 3 minutes.

2. Add orange juice, broth and gin to chicken mixture; cook, stirring occasionally, until chicken is cooked through. Remove chicken to serving platter; set aside and keep warm.

3. Continue to cook mixture remaining in skillet until slightly thickened and reduced to about ½ cup, stirring occasionally. Pour mixture over chicken; serve garnished with orange slices.

Each serving provides: 1 Fat; ½ Fruit; 2 Proteins; 30 Optional Calories

Per serving: 174 Calories; 17 g Protein; 6 g Fat; 8 g Carbohydrate; 33 mg Calcium; 50 mg Sodium; 41 mg Cholesterol; 1 g Dietary Fiber

CREOLE CHICKEN

This classic Creole dish is surprisingly simple to make. Serve it on a bed of white rice for an attractive presentation.

Makes 4 servings

1 teaspoon olive oil	¼ cup low-sodium chicken broth
10 ounces skinless boneless chicken thighs, cut into 8 equal pieces	2 teaspoons wine vinegar
	1 bay leaf
	1 teaspoon dried thyme leaves
1 cup diced onions	½ teaspoon salt
½ cup finely diced celery	½ teaspoon black pepper
½ cup diced green bell pepper	2 cups hot cooked long-grain rice
1 cup drained canned Italian tomatoes, coarsely chopped	
½ cup (4 fluid ounces) dry white wine	

1. In medium skillet, heat oil; add chicken. Cook over medium heat 2 minutes on each side, until golden brown. Remove chicken from skillet; set aside.
2. To same skillet, add onions, celery and green pepper; cook, stirring frequently, 4–5 minutes, until onions are golden brown. Add tomatoes, wine, broth, vinegar, bay leaf, thyme, salt and black pepper. Bring liquid to a boil, scraping up browned bits from bottom of skillet; cook, stirring frequently, until mixture is reduced by about a third.
3. Add reserved chicken to tomato mixture; stir to combine. Reduce heat to low; simmer, covered, 10–15 minutes, stirring occasionally, until chicken is cooked through. Remove and discard bay leaf.
4. To serve, spoon rice onto serving platter; top with chicken mixture.

Each serving provides: ¼ Fat; 1½ Vegetables; 2 Proteins; 1 Bread; 25 Optional Calories

Per serving: 284 Calories; 18 g Protein; 5 g Fat; 37 g Carbohydrate; 64 mg Calcium; 454 mg Sodium; 59 mg Cholesterol; 2 g Dietary Fiber

CHICKEN ANDOUILLE

This sauté is lightning-fast to make and really delicious! If you can't find th
Cajun staple, andouille sausage, kielbasa (Polish sausage) makes a fine subst
tute.

Makes 4 servings

2 teaspoons olive oil

13 ounces skinless boneless
chicken breasts, cut into
8 equal pieces

1 cup sliced onions

2 garlic cloves, minced

½ cup low-sodium chicken broth

¼ cup (2 fluid ounces) dry white
wine

2 tablespoons + 1 teaspoon
white wine vinegar

½ teaspoon dried thyme leaves

2 ounces cooked andouille
sausage, cut into ¼" thick
slices

¼ cup minced fresh flat-leaf
parsley

¼ teaspoon coarsely ground
black pepper

1. In medium skillet, heat oil; add chicken. Cook over medium-high hea
2 minutes on each side, until golden brown. Remove chicken from skille
set aside.
2. To same skillet, add onions; cook, stirring frequently, 4–5 minutes, unt
golden brown. Add garlic; cook, stirring constantly, 1 minute longer.
3. Add broth, wine and vinegar to onion mixture; bring liquid to a boil ove
high heat. Add reserved chicken, the thyme and sausage; cook, basting mea
frequently with pan juices, until chicken is cooked through and liquid
reduced to about ½ cup. Stir in parsley and pepper.

Each serving provides: ½ Fat; ½ Vegetable; 3 Proteins; 15 Optional Calorie

Per serving: 200 Calories; 24 g Protein; 7 g Fat; 5 g Carbohydrate; 37 mg
Calcium; 223 mg Sodium; 63 mg Cholesterol; 1 g Dietary Fiber

11

Treasures from the Far East

Sesame Chicken
Asian Lemon Chicken
Broiled Lemon Chicken
Chinese Red-Cooked Chicken
Steamed Chicken Dumplings
Chicken Udon
Yakitori
Japanese Chicken
Chicken Pad Thai
Tandoori Chicken
Chicken Satay
Chicken Curry
Coconut Chicken
Chicken Biriyani
One-Dish Indian Chicken and Cauliflower

SESAME CHICKEN

Sake—a dry Japanese rice wine—and ginger give this chicken dish its ligh spirited taste, while the sesame sauce lends a nutty flavor. Serve this flavorf dish with rice or noodles.

Makes 4 servings

One 1-pound chicken breast, skinned

½ teaspoon salt

2 tablespoons (1 fluid ounce) sake*

2 teaspoons ginger juice†

1 medium scallion, sliced and crushed

1 garlic clove, crushed

1 tablespoon + 1½ teaspoons sesame seeds

½ cup low-sodium chicken brot

2 teaspoons fresh lemon juice

1½ teaspoons low-sodium soy sauce

1 teaspoon firmly packed light or dark brown sugar

2 tablespoons fresh cilantro leaves

1. With sharp knife, make several slashes on skinned side of chicken breas rub chicken all over with ¼ teaspoon of the salt. Spray large heatproof pla with nonstick cooking spray (plate should fit into large saucepan). Plac chicken on prepared plate. Sprinkle chicken with sake and ginger juice, the top with scallion and garlic; refrigerate, covered, 2–4 hours.

2. Set a steamer rack or round baking rack into large saucepan; add 1–2" wa ter, being careful that water does not reach top of rack.

3. Bring water in saucepan to a boil; reduce heat. Uncover chicken mixtur place plate on rack. Cover saucepan; cook chicken over simmering wat 15–20 minutes, until just cooked through.

4. Remove chicken from saucepan, discarding scallion and garlic; set chicke aside to cool.

5. While chicken is cooling, in small skillet, toast sesame seeds over low hea stirring frequently, 1–2 minutes, until golden brown; transfer to food pr cessor. Add broth, lemon juice, soy sauce, brown sugar and the remainin ¼ teaspoon salt; process until well combined. Add cilantro; process 10 sec onds longer.

6. Remove and discard bones from cooled chicken, then slice thinly. Divid chicken evenly among 4 plates; top with sesame seed mixture.

Each serving provides: 2 Proteins; 30 Optional Calories

Per serving: 131 Calories; 18 g Protein; 4 g Fat; 3 g Carbohydrate; 46 mg Calcium; 372 mg Sodium; 48 mg Cholesterol; 0 g Dietary Fiber

*Sake, a dry Japanese rice wine, can be purchased in most liquor stores. If not available, substitute dry white wine or sherry.

† To make ginger juice, pare a large piece of fresh ginger. With a fine grater, grate ginger onto a plate; squeeze grated pulp to extract juice. Discard pulp.

ASIAN LEMON CHICKEN

Makes 4 servings

2 tablespoons (1 fluid ounce) dry sherry

1 tablespoon low-sodium soy sauce

Four 3-ounce skinless boneless chicken breasts

½ cup low-sodium chicken broth

2 tablespoons fresh lemon juice

2 teaspoons cornstarch

2 teaspoons Asian sesame oil*

1 tablespoon chopped pared fresh ginger root

1. In medium bowl, combine sherry and soy sauce; add chicken, tossing to coat thoroughly. Let stand 10 minutes.
2. In small bowl, combine broth, lemon juice and cornstarch, stirring until cornstarch is dissolved; set aside.
3. In large nonstick saucepan, heat oil; add ginger root. Cook, stirring constantly, 2 minutes. Add chicken; cook 2 minutes on each side, until golden brown. Stir in broth mixture; bring liquid to a boil. Cook, stirring frequently, 1 minute, until liquid thickens slightly.

Each serving provides: ½ Fat; 2 Proteins; 15 Optional Calories

Per serving: 139 Calories; 20 g Protein; 4 g Fat; 4 g Carbohydrate; 12 mg Calcium; 213 mg Sodium; 49 mg Cholesterol; 0 g Dietary Fiber

*Asian sesame oil can be purchased in Asian food stores or the Asian food section of some supermarkets.

BROILED LEMON CHICKEN

Makes 4 servings

Chicken:

- 1 egg white
- 1 tablespoon cornstarch
- 1 teaspoon low-sodium soy sauce
- ¾ teaspoon granulated sugar
- ⅛ teaspoon double-acting baking powder
- Four 3-ounce skinless boneless chicken breasts

Sauce:

- ⅓ cup low-sodium chicken broth
- 3 tablespoons fresh lemon juice
- 2 teaspoons granulated sugar
- 1 garlic clove, minced
- ½ teaspoon low-sodium soy sauce
- 1 teaspoon cornstarch, dissolved in 1 tablespoon cold water
- 1 medium scallion, thinly sliced
- 4 lemon slices to garnish

1. To prepare chicken, in medium bowl, with wire whisk, combine egg white, cornstarch, soy sauce, sugar and baking powder, blending until cornstarch is dissolved. Add chicken, tossing well to coat thoroughly. Refrigerate, covered, 1 hour.

2. Preheat broiler. Line large baking sheet with foil; spray with nonstick cooking spray.

3. In large pot, bring 4 quarts water to a boil over high heat; reduce heat to low. Add chicken; cook 30 seconds, until chicken pieces turn white. With skimmer or slotted spoon, remove chicken from water quickly; set aside to drain.

4. Place chicken on prepared baking sheet; broil 6" from heat 2 minutes on each side, until golden brown and cooked through.

5. To prepare sauce, in medium bowl, combine broth, lemon juice, sugar, garlic and soy sauce; bring to a boil. Stir in dissolved cornstarch; cook, stirring constantly, 1 minute, until mixture is slightly thickened.

6. To serve, arrange chicken on serving platter. Top chicken with sauce; sprinkle with scallions. Serve garnished with lemon slices.

Each serving provides: 2 Proteins; 25 Optional Calories

Per serving: 129 Calories; 21 g Protein; 1 g Fat; 7 g Carbohydrate; 22 mg Calcium; 138 mg Sodium; 49 mg Cholesterol; 0 g Dietary Fiber

CHINESE RED-COOKED CHICKEN

Rich, full of flavor, yet easy to make, this slow-cooked dish is delicious served over rice.

Makes 4 servings

½ cup low-sodium soy sauce

3 tablespoons (1½ fluid ounces) dry sherry

2 tablespoons firmly packed light or dark brown sugar

1 small mild or hot chili pepper

Three 3 × ½" strips orange zest*

3 slices pared fresh ginger root

2 garlic cloves

1 cinnamon stick

1 pound 8 ounces chicken parts, skinned

1 tablespoon cornstarch, dissolved in 2 tablespoons cold water

1. In medium saucepan, combine soy sauce, ½ cup water, the sherry, brown sugar, chili pepper, orange zest, ginger, garlic and cinnamon stick, stirring until sugar is dissolved; add chicken. Bring liquid to a boil; reduce heat to low. Cook, covered, 30 minutes, until chicken is cooked through and juices run clear when pierced with a fork. With slotted spoon, remove chicken to serving plate; keep warm.
2. Strain liquid into small bowl, discarding solids; return liquid to saucepan. Bring liquid to a boil; stir in dissolved cornstarch. Return mixture to a boil; cook 2 minutes, until slightly thickened. Pour over warm chicken.

Each serving provides: 2 Proteins; 40 Optional Calories

Per serving: 173 Calories; 16 g Protein; 4 g Fat; 13 g Carbohydrate; 20 mg Calcium; 833 mg Sodium; 50 mg Cholesterol; 0 g Dietary Fiber

The zest of the orange is the peel without any of the pith (white membrane). To remove zest from orange, use a zester or vegetable peeler; wrap orange in plastic wrap and refrigerate for use at another time.

STEAMED CHICKEN DUMPLINGS

Makes 4 servings

Dipping Sauce:

3 tablespoons low-sodium soy sauce

1 tablespoon + 1½ teaspoons rice wine vinegar or cider vinegar

1½ teaspoons granulated sugar

Dumplings:

10 ounces ground chicken

⅓ cup minced scallions

2 tablespoons chopped fresh cilantro leaves

2 teaspoons low-sodium soy sauce

2 teaspoons minced pared fresh ginger root

3 garlic cloves, minced

¼ cup low-sodium chicken broth

20 wonton skins (3 × 3" squares)*

1. To prepare dipping sauce, in small bowl, combine soy sauce, vinegar and sugar, stirring until sugar is dissolved; cover and set aside.
2. To prepare dumplings, in medium bowl, combine chicken, scallions, cilantro, soy sauce, ginger and garlic; stir in broth.
3. Spoon an equal amount of chicken mixture onto each wonton skin, placing each portion slightly below and to the right of center. Brush bottom and right edges of each square with water. Fold dry edges over to meet wet edges to form triangles; press lightly to seal.
4. Set a steamer rack or round baking rack into large saucepan; add 1–2" water, being careful that water does not reach top of rack. Spray large heatproof plate with nonstick cooking spray (plate should fit into saucepan).
5. Bring water in saucepan to a boil; reduce heat. Place dumplings in a single layer on prepared plate (if all dumplings do not fit on plate, work in batches); set plate on rack. Cook dumplings over simmering water, covered, 6 minutes, until wonton skins are translucent and filling is cooked and firm.
6. To serve, arrange 5 dumplings on each of 4 plates; divide dipping sauce evenly among 4 individual cups or small bowls. Serve dumplings with sauce.

Each serving provides: ¼ Vegetable; 2 Proteins; 1 Bread; 5 Optional Calories

Per serving: 248 Calories; 17 g Protein; 7 g Fat; 28 g Carbohydrate; 49 mg Calcium; 650 mg Sodium; 62 mg Cholesterol; 0 g Dietary Fiber

*Wonton skins can be purchased in Asian food stores or in the dairy, produce or frozen food section of some supermarkets.

Chicken Udon

Makes 4 servings

4 cups low-sodium chicken broth

8 ounces skinless boneless chicken thighs, cut into ½" pieces

1 medium carrot, halved lengthwise, thinly sliced

½ cup thinly sliced scallions

2 cups thoroughly washed and drained spinach leaves, shredded

4 ounces firm tofu, cubed

3 ounces udon noodles, cooked and drained*

1 tablespoon low-sodium soy sauce

2 teaspoons Asian sesame oil

2 teaspoons rice wine vinegar

1. In large saucepan, bring broth to a boil; reduce heat to low. Add chicken, carrot and scallions; cook 5 minutes, until chicken is just cooked through.
2. Add spinach, tofu, noodles, soy sauce, oil and vinegar to broth mixture; cook, stirring occasionally, 3 minutes longer, until spinach is wilted.

Each serving provides: ½ Fat; 1¾ Vegetables; 2 Proteins; 1 Bread; 20 Optional Calories

Per serving: 263 Calories; 22 g Protein; 10 g Fat; 23 g Carbohydrate; 114 mg Calcium; 241 mg Sodium; 67 mg Cholesterol; 2 g Dietary Fiber

Udon noodles, sometimes called wheat noodles, can be purchased in Asian food stores or the Asian food section of some supermarkets. They are sold in packages similar to those for spaghetti; if unavailable, substitute fettuccine or spaghetti.

YAKITORI

Serve this Japanese specialty with hot rice and a cucumber salad.

Makes 4 servings

¼ cup low-sodium soy sauce

2 tablespoons (1 fluid ounce) sake*

2 tablespoons (1 fluid ounce) mirin†

1½ teaspoons granulated sugar

10 ounces skinless boneless chicken breasts, cut into ¾" pieces

1 medium red bell pepper, seeded and cut into 1" chunks

4 medium scallions, trimmed

¼ teaspoon crushed red pepper flakes

¼ teaspoon coarsely ground black pepper

¼ teaspoon grated orange peel

½ teaspoon sesame seeds

1. Place four 8" wooden skewers in water; set aside until ready to use.
2. In medium bowl, with wire whisk, combine soy sauce, sake, mirin and sugar blending until sugar is dissolved; remove and set aside ½ of mixture for dipping sauce. To remaining mixture, add chicken, red pepper and scallion tossing well to coat thoroughly; refrigerate, covered, 1 hour.
3. Preheat broiler. Line large baking sheet with foil; spray with nonstick cooking spray.
4. Alternately thread ¼ of the chicken and pepper pieces and 1 scallion onto each skewer; reserve any soy sauce mixture remaining in bowl. Arrange skewers on prepared baking sheet; broil 6" from heat 2–3 minutes; turn Baste with reserved soy sauce mixture; broil 2 minutes longer, until chicken and vegetables are golden brown and chicken is cooked through.
5. In small bowl, combine crushed red pepper flakes, ground black pepper and orange peel; sprinkle evenly over skewers, then sprinkle evenly with sesame seeds. Serve with reserved dipping sauce.

Each serving provides: ¾ Vegetable; 2 Proteins; 25 Optional Calories

Per serving: 131 Calories; 17 g Protein; 1 g Fat; 8 g Carbohydrate; 21 mg Calcium; 438 mg Sodium; 41 mg Cholesterol; 1 g Dietary Fiber

*Sake, a dry Japanese rice wine, can be purchased in most liquor stores. If not available, substitute dry white wine or sherry.

† Mirin, a thick, syrupy, sweet Japanese wine, sometimes labeled as sweet cooking rice wine, can e purchased in some liquor stores, Japanese food stores or the Asian food section of some supermarkets.

JAPANESE CHICKEN

This sweet and pungent chicken dish is equally good hot or cold. In the summertime, try cooking it on the grill.

Makes 4 servings

1 tablespoon + 1½ teaspoons low-sodium soy sauce

1 tablespoon + 1½ teaspoons low-sodium chicken broth or water

1 tablespoon honey

1 teaspoon ginger juice*

1 teaspoon fresh lemon juice

10 ounces skinless boneless chicken thighs, cut into 4 equal pieces

Lemon slices to garnish

1. To prepare marinade, in gallon-size sealable plastic bag, combine soy sauce, broth, honey, ginger juice and lemon juice; add chicken. Seal bag, squeezing out air; turn to coat chicken thoroughly. Refrigerate at least 2 hours or overnight, turning bag occasionally.
2. Preheat broiler. Remove chicken from bag; discard marinade. Broil chicken 6" from heat, 3½ minutes on each side, until chicken is cooked through and juices run clear when pierced with a fork. Serve hot, at room temperature or chilled, garnished with lemon slices.

Each serving provides: 2 Proteins; 15 Optional Calories

Per serving: 104 Calories; 14 g Protein; 3 g Fat; 5 g Carbohydrate; 8 mg Calcium; 209 mg Sodium; 59 mg Cholesterol; 0 g Dietary Fiber

*To make ginger juice, pare a large piece of fresh ginger. With a fine grater, grate ginger onto a late; squeeze grated pulp to extract juice. Discard pulp.

Chicken Pad Thai

Makes 4 servings

1 egg white

1 tablespoon cornstarch

1 tablespoon (½ fluid ounce) dry sherry

¼ teaspoon salt

9 ounces skinless boneless chicken thighs, cut into 1" pieces

½ cup low-sodium chicken broth

2 garlic cloves, minced

3 tablespoons Asian fish sauce*

1 tablespoon + 1½ teaspoons ketchup

1 tablespoon granulated sugar

2 teaspoons fresh lime juice

1 tablespoon chopped fresh cilantro leaves

2 cups shredded Chinese cabbage

2 cups cooked cellophane noodles*

½ cup sliced scallions

1 ounce coarsely chopped unsalted peanuts

1. In medium bowl, with wire whisk, combine egg white, cornstarch, sherry and salt, blending until cornstarch is dissolved; add chicken, tossing well to coat thoroughly. Refrigerate, covered, 1 hour.
2. In large pot, bring 4 quarts water to a boil over high heat; reduce heat to low. In batches, add chicken, a few pieces at a time, to simmering water; cook 30 seconds, until chicken pieces turn white. With skimmer or slotted spoon, remove chicken from water quickly; set aside to drain.
3. In medium skillet, combine broth and garlic; bring liquid to a boil. Reduce heat to low; add chicken. Cook 4 minutes, until chicken is just cooked through. With skimmer or slotted spoon, remove chicken from broth mixture; set aside to drain.
4. In large bowl, with wire whisk, combine fish sauce, ketchup, sugar and lime juice; stir in cilantro. Add cabbage and cellophane noodles, tossing well to combine thoroughly. Add chicken; toss again to combine.
5. To serve, transfer chicken mixture to serving platter; sprinkle with scallions and peanuts.

Each serving provides: ½ Fat; 1¼ Vegetables; 2 Proteins; 1 Bread; 35 Optional Calories

er serving: 270 Calories; 18 g Protein; 7 g Fat; 32 g Carbohydrate; 61 mg Calcium; 280 mg Sodium (does not include Asian fish sauce—data unavailable); 53 mg Cholesterol; 1 g Dietary Fiber

*Asian fish sauce and cellophane noodles can be purchased in Asian food stores or the Asian food ction of some supermarkets.

ANDOORI CHICKEN

lthough this Indian specialty is traditionally made in a super-hot tandoori oven, ou can get great results in your own kitchen.

Makes 4 servings

1½ cups plain nonfat yogurt	½ teaspoon ground ginger
2 teaspoons mild or hot chili powder	½ teaspoon ground cardamom
1 teaspoon ground cumin	8 ounces chicken breast, skinned
1 teaspoon ground coriander	8 ounces chicken drumsticks, skinned
1 teaspoon ground turmeric	1 cup chopped tomatoes
¾ teaspoon salt	

1. In large bowl, with wire whisk, combine yogurt, chili powder, cumin, coriander, turmeric, salt, ginger and cardamom; transfer 1 cup mixture to small bowl. Add chicken to remaining yogurt mixture; toss well to coat thoroughly. Refrigerate both mixtures, covered, overnight.
2. Preheat oven to 450° F.
3. Place chicken in an 8" square baking pan; top with any remaining yogurt mixture in large bowl. Bake 15 minutes, until chicken is cooked through and juices run clear when pierced with a fork.
4. Remove chicken meat from bones; discard bones. Cut chicken into bite-size pieces; divide evenly among 4 plates. Spoon ¼ of reserved yogurt mixture alongside each portion of chicken; top each with an equal amount of tomatoes.

ach serving provides: ½ Milk; ½ Vegetable; 2 Proteins

er serving: 168 Calories; 22 g Protein; 4 g Fat; 10 g Carbohydrate; 192 mg Calcium; 541 mg Sodium; 52 mg Cholesterol; 1 g Dietary Fiber

CHICKEN SATAY

Makes 4 servings

Chicken:

1 medium scallion, minced

2 tablespoons low-sodium soy sauce

1 tablespoon + 1 teaspoon fresh lime juice

1 tablespoon firmly packed light or dark brown sugar

2 garlic cloves, minced

10 ounces skinless boneless chicken thighs, cut into ¾" pieces

Peanut Sauce:

2 teaspoons creamy peanut butter

¼ teaspoon firmly packed light or dark brown sugar

¼ teaspoon fresh lime juice

1 medium scallion, minced

2 tablespoons low-sodium chicken broth

1 tablespoon low-sodium soy sauce

⅛ teaspoon ground red pepper, or to taste

1. Preheat broiler. Line large baking sheet with foil; spray with nonstick cooking spray. Place four 8" wooden skewers in water; set aside until ready to use.

2. To prepare chicken, in medium bowl, with wire whisk, combine scallion, soy sauce, lime juice, brown sugar and garlic, blending until sugar is dissolved; add chicken, tossing well to coat thoroughly. Let stand 10 minutes.

3. To prepare sauce, in small bowl, with wire whisk, combine peanut butter, brown sugar and lime juice, blending well until sugar is dissolved; continuing to whisk, add scallion, broth, soy sauce and red pepper. Set aside.

4. Thread ¼ of the chicken onto each skewer; reserve any soy sauce mixture remaining in bowl. Place skewers on prepared baking sheet; broil 6" from heat 2–3 minutes; turn. Baste with reserved soy sauce mixture; broil 2 minutes longer, until chicken is golden brown and cooked through.

5. To serve, spoon ¼ of the peanut sauce onto each of 4 plates; top each with 1 skewer of chicken.

Each serving provides: ½ Fat; 2 Proteins; 15 Optional Calories

Per serving: 126 Calories; 15 g Protein; 4 g Fat; 6 g Carbohydrate; 17 mg Calcium; 370 mg Sodium; 59 mg Cholesterol; 0 g Dietary Fiber

CHICKEN CURRY

Makes 4 servings

3 tablespoons shredded coconut
2 teaspoons vegetable oil
10 ounces skinless boneless chicken thighs, cut into 1" pieces
½ cup chopped onion
1 small McIntosh apple, cored, pared and thinly sliced
2 garlic cloves, crushed

2 teaspoons chopped pared fresh ginger root
1 cup low-sodium chicken broth
½ medium banana, thinly sliced
2 teaspoons tomato paste
1 teaspoon mild or hot curry powder, or to taste
2 cups hot cooked long-grain rice

1. In small bowl, combine coconut and ¾ cup boiling water; let stand 30 minutes. Strain, squeezing coconut to extract as much liquid as possible; reserve liquid, discarding solids.

2. In large nonstick skillet, heat oil; add chicken. Cook over medium-high heat, stirring frequently, 4 minutes, until golden brown. Remove chicken from skillet; set aside.

3. To same skillet, add onion, apple, garlic and ginger; reduce heat to medium. Cook, stirring frequently, 4 minutes, until mixture is lightly browned. Stir in ¼ cup of the broth; cook 4 minutes, until liquid has evaporated. Stir in banana, tomato paste, curry powder, the remaining ¾ cup broth and the reserved coconut liquid; bring liquid to a boil. Reduce heat to low; simmer 5 minutes, until flavors are blended. Remove from heat; let cool slightly.

4. Transfer mixture to blender; purée until smooth. Return mixture to skillet; stir in chicken. Cook over low heat, stirring occasionally, 3 minutes, until chicken is cooked through. Serve over rice.

Each serving provides: ½ Fat; ½ Fruit; ¼ Vegetable; 2 Proteins; 1 Bread; 15 Optional Calories

Per serving: 302 Calories; 18 g Protein; 7 g Fat; 41 g Carbohydrate; 31 mg Calcium; 108 mg Sodium; 59 mg Cholesterol; 2 g Dietary Fiber

COCONUT CHICKEN

These crunchy drumsticks are great for parties as well as for family dinners.

Makes 4 servings

3 tablespoons shredded coconut

3 tablespoons all-purpose flour

½ teaspoon salt

¼ teaspoon ground allspice

¼ teaspoon ground red pepper

1 pound 8 ounces roaster chicken-wing drumsticks, skinned*

2 egg whites, lightly beaten with 2 teaspoons water

¾ cup low-sodium chicken broth

¼ cup mango chutney†

½ teaspoon Dijon-style mustard

1 medium scallion, minced

½ small mango, peeled, pitted and diced

1. Preheat oven to 450° F. Spray large baking sheet with nonstick cooking spray.
2. In food processor or blender, combine coconut, flour, salt, allspice and ⅛ teaspoon of the red pepper; purée until well combined. Transfer mixture to sheet of wax paper or a paper plate. Place egg white mixture in shallow bowl.
3. Dip each chicken wing into egg white mixture, then coconut mixture, turning to coat well. Place chicken on prepared baking sheet; bake 25 minutes until cooked through and golden brown.
4. In small skillet, bring broth to a boil; stir in chutney, Dijon mustard and the remaining ⅛ teaspoon red pepper. Cook, stirring occasionally, 2 minutes. Stir in scallion; remove from heat. Add mango; stir to combine.
5. To serve, divide mango mixture evenly among 4 plates; top each with ¼ the chicken.

Each serving provides: ¼ Fruit; 2 Proteins; ¼ Bread; 55 Optional Calories

Per serving: 231 Calories; 20 g Protein; 6 g Fat; 22 g Carbohydrate; 17 mg Calcium; 568 mg Sodium; 48 mg Cholesterol; 1 g Dietary Fiber

---

Roaster chicken wings, with the drumstick portion already separated from the lower part of the wing, are available in the meat section of the supermarket. Freeze the lower part to have on hand when making chicken broth.

†Mango chutney can be purchased in the gourmet food section of most supermarkets.*

CKEN BIRIYANI

richly spiced Indian rice dish is studded with plump, tender pieces of ken. If basmati rice is not available, substitute long-grain rice.

zes 4 servings

medium onion, cut into large chunks	½ teaspoon ground turmeric
garlic cloves	½ teaspoon ground cumin
One ½" slice pared fresh ginger root	¼ teaspoon black pepper
cup plain nonfat yogurt	¼ teaspoon ground cardamom
cup fresh cilantro leaves	10 ounces skinless boneless chicken breasts, cut into ½" pieces
tablespoons fresh lemon juice	4 ounces uncooked basmati rice*
teaspoon salt	

In food processor or blender, combine onion, garlic and ginger; purée until smooth. Add yogurt, cilantro, lemon juice, ¼ teaspoon of the salt, the turmeric, cumin, pepper and cardamom; process until well combined. Transfer mixture to gallon-size sealable plastic bag; add chicken. Seal bag, squeezing out air; turn to coat chicken. Refrigerate at least 2 hours or over-night, turning bag occasionally.

In large saucepan, combine rice, 1⅓ cups water and remaining ¼ teaspoon salt; bring water to a boil. Reduce heat to low; cook, covered, 10 minutes, until rice begins to soften.

Add chicken mixture to rice; increase heat to medium-high. Bring liquid to a boil; reduce heat to low. Simmer, covered, 20 minutes, until chicken is cooked through and rice is tender.

serving provides: ¼ Milk; ¼ Vegetable; 2 Proteins; 1 Bread; 10 Optional Calories

serving: 220 Calories; 23 g Protein; 2 g Fat; 30 g Carbohydrate; 135 mg Calcium; 377 mg Sodium; 42 mg Cholesterol; 1 g Dietary Fiber

*Basmati rice is a fragrant, fine-grained rice from India. It can be purchased in specialty shops gourmet food section of some supermarkets.

One-Dish Indian Chicken and Cauliflower

Potatoes and cauliflower are often paired in Indian cuisine. Here, they are coo[k]
in broth and combined with chicken to make a delicious, one-pot meal.

Makes 4 servings

1 tablespoon + 1 teaspoon olive oil

1 medium onion, chopped

1 tablespoon chopped pared fresh ginger root

2 garlic cloves, slivered

2 cups cauliflower florets

10 ounces pared Idaho potatoes, cut into ¾" cubes

1½ teaspoons ground turmeric

¾ teaspoon salt

½ teaspoon minced fresh hot chili pepper

1 cup canned crushed tomat[o]

⅓ cup chopped fresh cilantro leaves

10 ounces skinless boneless chicken thighs, cut into 1" pieces

1 tablespoon fresh lemon jui[ce]

1. In large nonstick skillet or shallow Dutch oven, heat oil; add onion, gi[nger] and garlic. Cook over medium heat, stirring occasionally, 2–3 minutes, [until] onion is softened. Add cauliflower, potatoes, turmeric, salt and chili [pep]per; cook, stirring frequently, 4 minutes. Add 1 cup water; bring liqu[id to] a boil. Reduce heat to low; simmer, covered, 25 minutes.

2. Stir tomatoes and cilantro into cauliflower mixture; cook, covered, 10 [min]utes. Add chicken; stir to combine. Cook, covered, 10 minutes longer, [until] chicken is cooked through; stir in lemon juice.

Each serving provides: 1 Fat; 1¾ Vegetables; 2 Proteins; ½ Bread

Per serving: 220 Calories; 17 g Protein; 8 g Fat; 21 g Carbohydrate; 55 m[g] Calcium; 584 mg Sodium; 59 mg Cholesterol; 3 g Dietary Fiber

Glossary and
Mail Order Sources

")SSARY

n chili paste: A spicy paste, which can be purchased in Asian food stores or
e Asian food section of some supermarkets.

n fish sauce: A thin, salty brown sauce, which can be purchased in Asian
 stores or in the Asian food section of some supermarkets.

kwheat soba noodles: Very fine Japanese noodles, which can be purchased
 ian food stores or in some health food stores.

ophane noodles: Fine, transparent noodles made from the starch of green
g beans, which can be purchased in Asian food stores or in the Asian food
on of some supermarkets.

ese chili sauce: A spicy sauce made from chilies, salt and vinegar, which
 e purchased in Asian food stores or in the Asian food section of some su-
arkets.

ented black beans: Beans with a salty, winelike flavor, which can be pur-
ed in Asian food stores or in the Asian food section of some supermarkets.

es de Provence: An herb blend typical of southern France, which usually
oines thyme, bay leaf, rosemary, sage, savory, fennel and/or marjoram. It
e puchased in gourmet stores.

in sauce: A spicy-sweet sauce made from soy beans, garlic and spices, which
e purchased in Asian food markets or in the Asian food section of some
rmarkets.

Mirin: A sweet Japanese cooking wine, which can be purchased in Asian stores or in some liquor stores.

Oyster sauce: A thick, dark brown, mildly fishy sauce, which can be purch in Asian food stores or in the Asian food section of some supermarkets.

Sake: A Japanese rice wine, which can be purchased in Asian food stores ai some liquor stores. If unavailable, substitute brandy or sherry.

Szechuan peppercorns: Reddish brown berries with a spicy, piney flavor, w can be purchased in Asian food stores or in the Asian food section of som permarkets.

Udon noodles: Thick Japanese noodles made from wheat flour, which ca purchased in Asian food stores or in the Asian food section of some super kets.

Zest: The peel of citrus fruit without any of the pith (white membrane). T move zest from an orange, lemon or lime, use a zester or vegetable peeler. \ fruit in plastic wrap and refrigerate for use at another time.

MAIL ORDER SOURCES

ANZEM Importers
10301 S. E. Stark, Portland, OR 97267 (503) 253-9985

Oriental Food Market
2801 West Howard Street, Chicago, IL 60645 (312) 274-2826
($2.00 for catalog, refundable with first purchase)

Spice Merchant
P.O. Box 524, Jackson Hole, WY 83001 (800) 551-5999 or (307) 551-5

Uwajimaya
519 Sixth Avenue South, Seattle, WA 98104 (800) 889-1928; in
Washington state, (206) 624-6248